Firebird
Odyssey

by

Mark J. Villarino

MJV Enterprises Ltd., Inc.

For further information, please address:

> MJV Enterprises Ltd., Inc.
> 14011 Clarkdale Avenue #2188
> Norwalk, CA 90650

The paper used in this publication meets the minimum standard requirements of American National Standard for Information Sciences — Permanence of Paper for Printed Library Materials, ANSI Z39.48-1984.
Printed in the United States of America by KindleDirect, an http://Amazon.com company.
ISBN: 979-8-7551-2890-2
Bibliographic cataloging information:

Author	Mark J. Villarino.
Main title	Firebird Odyssey
Published/created	MJV Enterprises ltd., Inc.
Description	22 cm.
Subject	Non-fiction.

Contents

Introduction

I am proud to acknowledge the invaluable insight and creativity that my dear long-time friend Keith Rideau brought to this project. Thanks dude. I also need to thank Kerri Jackson for her encouragement and support of this project.

This is going to sound uncharacteristically narcissistic and even as I'm writing this I'm thinking, 'Man, I must be completely full of myself for doing this'. But, here goes...

Friends and acquaintances have been flattering me for years saying that they like the way I tell stories, and sometimes they even say they also like the story itself. I don't know when or where my skill for story-telling came from, let alone how I cultivated my gift of gab. On one of my trips to Ireland, I did, indeed, kiss the Blarney Stone but I had been orating tales long before then.

I recently became aware that when a story pops into my head and needs to be told, I preface it with a question or statement containing the phrase "...the time when..." somewhere within. For instance, "Did I tell you about <u>the time when</u>...", "Do you remember <u>the time when</u>...", "That reminds me of <u>the time when</u>...". That's almost like how a lot of jokes start with, "A guy walks into a bar...". Anyway, although I enjoy storytelling, I'm reluctant to repeat myself or tell the same story twice to any one person. So, I quickly follow up with something like, "Please tell me if you've heard this and I won't repeat it; I really don't like to be redundant." Who wants to hear the same old story again and again, right? Despite that, some listeners have acknowledged that they have heard the story before but they like the way I tell it and want to hear it again. I think they're just being polite.

The way I tell stories is the way I would like to have them told to me. It's almost always rather intimate, usually one-on-one but with no more than four interlocutors; I by no means seek out sycophants. This close environment allows for questions to be asked and the storyteller & listeners to engage in dialogue. Furthermore, as I'm telling the story, I can look into the listener's eyes and tell if they understand what I'm saying. Most listeners are generally too polite to interrupt when they don't understand or miss something but their eyes betray their bewilderment. When I recognize those instances, I'll usually ask, "Know what I mean?", immediately followed by, "kinda like..." in order to explain or clarify without putting them on the spot. Moreover, I like to paint a picture so as to help the listener live the story as I re-live it myself. Sort of like transporting the listener to the time and place that the story happened by immersing them with descriptors and details. I make facial expressions, use my hands a lot and sometimes my whole body for illustration purposes, and I change the tone and timbre of my voice for the different characters. That's not feasible when writing stories out on paper. Like they say, a picture is worth a thousand words. For example, in person, I may have a photo with me, hold it up and say to some fellow antique car guys, who are my usual demographic, "When he opened his garage where he kept his model T, there was that smell you'd expect from an old garage." For the uninitiated, I'd have to write it out something like. "It was a typical afternoon in June here in California. He had an old one-car garage with a single lift-up style door. The outside of the garage was finished in a very light gray stucco and the wooden door & trim was terracotta colored. The paint on the wood parts was chipped and flaking in a number of places which led me to believe it had been some years since it was last painted. He unlocked the padlock on the left side of the door, lifted the aged steel latch, moved it to the right with a 'clunk' to unlock the door, hung the padlock back on the latch, then, stepping to the center of the door, grasped the handle and readied himself to open it. The hinges squeaked just a little and the springs lightly twanged as he pulled the door up, slowly revealing his beloved Ford model T. The air emanating from the garage filled my nostrils with the familiar nostalgic aroma of different automotive fluids and greases, with a subtle hint of leather which one associates with antique cars."

3

Well, you get the idea. On the one hand, writing the story out makes it way more verbose than relaying it orally and once it's written down, it becomes, for lack of a better term, rigid. What I mean by that is, telling a story live is very dynamic and vocal intonations as well as facial expressions communicate much more than words alone. Also, I can adjust certain details to better suit the listener, for instance, if it's a car freak, I can go into technical specifications and statistics whereas with non-car folks, I simplify it considerably otherwise they would get lost and quickly lose interest. On the other hand, once it's written, it will be preserved for posterity.

Anyway, I wrote this story the way I would tell it; in the first person. In other words, I'm *literally* telling you the story as though we were sitting across the table from each other having a couple of drinks, and as such, it's in natural speech with all the subtleties and nuances that distinguish it from grammatically correct proper written English. Another thing I did was to incorporate, so to speak, a music soundtrack. You see, music plays a vital role in most everyone's lives. When I was a teenager, my friends and I constantly listened to music and it was often the most important aspect in our lives during those turbulent adolescent years. The music spoke to us and made sense when our parents, teachers, and the rest of the world didn't. We weren't hung up on what the artist *meant* to communicate so much as how the music made us *feel*. We also didn't

4

think twice about spending money to buy recordings or tickets to shows. Some music influenced us, defined us, and much of it was like a soundtrack as our lives were taking shape and we were becoming adults. Now, well into adulthood, hearing pieces of that soundtrack transports me back to that time and place, and even evokes the same emotions and feelings. There are even times when listening to a certain song I haven't heard in a long time will inspire me to say, "Oh man, this song reminds me of the time when..." To help convey those feelings and emotions to you, I named several songs within the story which is the best way I could think of to add a "soundtrack".

Another element which I believe makes for a riveting story is when it's based on actual events. The story contained within these pages is an unvarnished telling of what actually happened during the Christmas season of 1987. Gas was about a buck per gallon and "pay at the pump" was only a year old so almost none of the stations had it; you had to pay an attendant, usually before you pumped, and the attendant knew how to do arithmetic and count-back money when giving change. The national speed limit was 55 mph. The only way to have easy 2-way mobile communication was to install a CB (citizen band) radio in your car. The CB was a one-time expense and it was free to use but you could only talk to other people who had a CB and its range was limited. Cellular telephones were a <u>very</u> expensive novelty that were the size of a brick, just about as heavy, and their batteries lasted no more than about a half-hour, however, pay-phones were everywhere. The first smart phone was still seven years away. Most people had telephone answering machines at home to record messages. People who needed or wanted immediate notification of a message would have pagers, also known as beepers. The possibility of sending or receiving a text wouldn't exist for another year and the first experimental text wouldn't be sent until late 1992. The internet was dominated by universities and AOL was still two years away. People had to interact face to face, speak over the phone, or write a letter, usually by hand. Navigation was done by a human reading a paper map; the first GPS navigation system was still two years away. The best radio you could get for your car was AM/FM Stereo; satellite radio was almost twenty years away. Photographs were done with a film camera or a Polaroid and video cameras were about twice the size of a loaf of bread. *Anything* digital was a really expensive novelty. Marijuana was illegal everywhere.

All the personages in this story are real but, because I do not have total recall, some of the names are fictitious.

I hope you enjoy reading this as much as I enjoyed reliving it while writing it.

There's no Place Like Home

You know, everyone has — or should have — that one "larger than life" grand adventure which, at the time it's happening, doesn't seem as spectacular as what you see in the movies until many years later when you ask a friend of yours, "Did I ever tell you about the time when I went halfway across country in a stolen Firebird?"

If I were to pitch this as a movie, I would say it's a coming of age, buddy, 1987 Christmas-time road-trip adventure with action, suspense, some comedy and some heartbreak, that has a bitter-sweet yet positive conclusion.

It features a car-chase, a couple run-ins with police... Know what? How 'bout I just tell you.

* * *

Right after I finished my final exams for the 1987 fall quarter during my second year at UCLA, I packed up a few things to catch the Green Tortoise bus to go home to Monterey for winter break. It was the night of Thursday, December 10, when a friend of mine drove me from the dorms to the bus stop which was at the Hostel California in Venice — long gone now — on the corner of Lincoln Blvd. and Lucille Ave. Little did I know my experience on this bus was to foreshadow how my winter break was about to unfold.

My first clue that this was an unconventional bus line should've been that this bus was departing at nine o'clock at night, or that it looked like a converted school bus, or that the seating included overhead-bunks — of which I took the one right behind the driver — and seats that folded down to become beds; 'This certainly is different', I thought to myself. But it didn't dawn on me just how different this bus line was until we started rolling and the driver announced that there was no drinking of alcohol or smoking of tobacco on the bus..., however, imbibing of 'herb' was only to be done on the freeway after we leave the county. To the mild disappointment — veiled in understanding — of my friends at home and in college, I never indulged in pot nor have I ever had the desire, but I don't mind hanging out with folks who do; they tend to be more interesting. The driver concluded his announcement by offering to play cassettes handed to him, with the exclusion of the Grateful Dead. Had I known about that, I would've brought some tapes; maybe had him play *Smokin'* by Boston.

* * *

8

So, the journey was shaping up to be a groovy one, except for one poor young man who had a look of terror on his face, as though something horrific was going to happen to him amongst all these college aged stoners. He sat as close to the front door as he could, right next to an open window so as to be supplied with non-stop fresh air. That dude was like *really* uptight. I think one of the first tunes the driver played was *In-A-Gadda-Da-Vida* by Iron Butterfly. Then there was the guy on the seat below my bunk who didn't have any weed but he did have a regular bottle of liquid paper which he huffed till he passed out then spilled all over himself. 'Ah', I thought to myself, 'That explains why I've been occasionally smelling xylene.' By the way, my major at UCLA was in chemistry. Yup, this was going to be an interesting "trip".

I slept most of the way, only waking up at rest stops where we could use a restroom, or at stops where passengers would embark and/or disembark. I couldn't help but notice that young mister "Uptight" didn't leave the bus until the driver did and didn't get back on the bus until the driver did. I don't think that dude slept a single wink, from which I derived a bit of schadenfreude, on the entire ride.

* * *

We arrived in Salinas the next morning where I gathered my things and disembarked — leaving Mr. Uptight to his fate — then, using a payphone, I called my mom to come pick me up. I was eager to get home, hang with my friends, and cruise in my beloved "Night Machine". I respectfully ask for your patience as I'm about to indulge in some testosterone fueled gearhead speak, after all, we guys can't help but to boast about our pride-and-joy.

The Night Machine was a green 1974 Chevrolet Monte Carlo Landau, fully loaded with power windows, power locks, power seat, cruise control, tilt-wheel, etc. I got the name from the Night Ranger song of the same name. I bought this car from a used car dealer for $500 back in early 1984. I had put in an engine I rebuilt myself featuring a 4-bolt main 350 small block bored 30-over, torque plate honed, forged steel crank, a pair of vintage double-hump "fuelie" heads I got from GM Sports Salvage in San Jose that were tricked out with 202 intake and 160 exhaust valves, Teflon valve stem seals, oversized valve springs with aluminum retainers, and polished ports. I installed an LT1 cam, 30-over pistons with molly rings, an Edelbrock performer intake manifold and a Rochester QJ I tweaked myself. I had the factory single exhaust upgraded to true dual exhaust with free-flow mufflers. I was in command of ~385 hp. I also cleaned up the body and repainted her myself, and put a Pioneer AM/FM stereo cassette in the dash with an external amplifier/equalizer which I mounted inside the glove-box, and, of course, JBL speakers. Hey, I was a young, red-blooded American college kid who wanted a cool car and since I couldn't afford to buy one already done, I had to build one with what I had available to me. As a side note, I still have that car and use it as my daily driver. I don't intend to ever let her go. Hmmm, the adventures I had with her could be sufficiently voluminous to be the basis of a series.

Anyway, the only place to go cruising in that area of California back in the mid-1980s was South Main Street in Salinas, a one-mile long stretch of road with two-lanes each way and a left-turn median flanked by dozens of eateries, shops, and some gas stations. So, right after I bought my car in 1984, most every Friday and Saturday night, my close friend Eric — the first friend I made after arriving at Fort Ord back when my mom got stationed there — and I would get in the Night Machine and cruise up and down South Main for action, be it chicks, house-party invites, or stop-light-to-stop-light races. Occasionally, some of our other friends would tag along like a guy we called "Smurf", Brett, a dude from Puerto Rico named Martin, Jay — all of whom I met through Eric —, and Noah, whom I met at Monterey Peninsula College (MPC); Eric, Brett, and Smurf were still in high school. Sometimes, we would cruise South Main in Jay's car. He had a stock base model 1978 Pontiac Firebird Esprit with the Red Bird trim package equipped with a 305ci V8. It was painted in Roman Red with a matching red interior and had a Gold pinstripe treatment with Red Bird graphics on the Bpillars. It also utilized the Trans-Am style steering wheel and dash except these were finished with gold spokes and a gold dash face which was unique to the Red Bird option, but it didn't have any of the performance trim commonly seen on the Trans Am such as the front and rear spoilers or T-top. Nevertheless, it was still an eye-catching car and did okay in the stop-light races. Noah had a cherry 1967 Camaro with a dark metallic blue paint job. Other than me, Noah was the only other guy in our crew who was in college. Though Noah's Camaro only had a straight-six in it, he beefed it up with an Offenhauser manifold, 4-barrel carb, and legit twin headers that fed a true dual exhaust system. That Camaro actually did pretty well in the stop-light races. After a quick sprint, when the other guy usually asked Noah about his V8, responding that it's a 250ci inline-six with a powerglide automatic... the look on the other guy's face was always priceless, saying, "You're running a straight-six?". Brett had a 1975 box stock Honda Civic CVCC 1488 which we called the "Lemon". When he got it, the paint was a faded oxidized yellow. One day back in 1985, Brett and I rubbed out the paint to reveal a bright canary yellow finish. It looked so good that some of the kids at his high school thought we had painted it over the weekend. We tossed around the idea of retrofitting it with a rear wheel drive chassis so he could run a V6 in it. As light as that car was, imagine how fast it would've been.

Cruising wasn't the only thing we did on the weekends. Sometimes, when we had a little more extra cash than usual, we would head up to the Santa Cruz beach boardwalk for the day and troll for foxes there. That's where I met this sweet hot chick, Makai, who helped me learn how to drink coffee, an acquired taste, at her favorite place; Ferrell's donut shop. The guys and I would also go to San Jose to Mother's, a 16-21 night club attached to Futurama Bowling Alley located on Stevens Creek Blvd at Lawrence Expressway. A few times, when we really felt ambitious, we would start the day off at the boardwalk in Santa Cruz then take highway 17 over the hill into San Jose to go to Mother's, not getting back home until around 3:00 am. Ferrell's is still there today but Mother's is long gone.

Ya know, recalling these times reminds me of the Bryan Adams song, *Summer of '69*, which was playing on the radio back then. Every time I hear that song today, I'm transported right back to those days in the Monterey, Santa Cruz, San Jose area; I can especially relate to the lyrics,

> Man we were killin' time
> We were young and restless
> We needed to unwind
> I guess nothin' can last forever...

* * *

So, after the summer of '87, I left Monterey for the fall quarter at UCLA and when I arrived back home for winter break after my adventurous bus ride, I got my Night Machine cleaned up, checked some stuff under the hood, started her up, played *Highway Star* by Deep Purple on the stereo, then sped off in search of my crew.

When living in the moment as we did back then — after all, it was known as the "me-first" decade —, you kind of lose perspective. There's a bumper-sticker I've seen that reads, "Kick your teenagers out while they still know everything." Coming home after my very first quarter away at college the year before — 1986 — was my first hard reality-check that, not only did I not know everything, in the grand design, my impact was essentially negligible. I didn't necessarily expect everything back home to be frozen in suspended animation while I was gone but I nevertheless felt rather disappointed and left out when I discovered that life had gone on without me being there. For instance, Brett got accepted to California State University Fresno and had moved there around the end of summer 1987 and his parents had moved out of California by that winter so he wasn't around anymore. I often wondered what sort of fun times I missed out on while I was away. The severity of that disappointment lessened a little bit each time I came back home from UCLA at the end of each successive quarter. It was still a bummer, though.

So, winter break '87, my first stop was Eric's house. His parents had split sometime during the past year and he was living with his father. His mother and sister had moved to Abilene Kansas where his mother's family lived. Eric's father, Rick, wasn't very much engaged in his life. While he was still in the army, he frequently went out in the field on training maneuvers leaving Eric to fend for himself. Jay had parental issues of his own at home so he spent many nights at Eric's, so many in fact that he practically lived there. He considered Eric to be his closest and most trusted friend. Unfortunately Jay was a misunderstood soul because he gave the impression of being a selfish wild child. Once you got past his gruff façade, he was an inherently decent guy. He helped Eric get a job at the same pizza parlor he worked at and, since Eric didn't drive, he would always give him a ride to work. He was also a loyal friend to Eric. When an employer they both worked for discharged one of them, the other would quit and they would both get another job somewhere else.

So, I called to make sure Eric was home before I drove over. When I arrived at his place, I parked out front, got out of my Night Machine, went up to the door and knocked. Eric came to the door.

"MARK! I'm so glad you're home on Christmas break."

"Me too, dude. How's it hangin'?"

"Come on in and I'll tell you all about it 'n' shit."

You'll be hearing that a lot; 'n' shit. We used it in place of 'and stuff' *all* the time.

As I stepped into Eric's house, I noticed almost all their furniture was gone and said, "*Dude*. You guys movin' 'n' shit?"

"Yeah we are. My dad's not re-upping so we hafta get out."

"Re-upping" means reenlisting in the army. I should've mentioned that Eric and the guys, myself included, except for Noah, were all army brats living on Fort Ord which was situated between the towns of Marina and Seaside in California. Fort Ord is now California State University Monterey Bay.

Eric went on, "My dad's gonna be takin' me to Clay Center, Kansas, man."

"Holy shit, dude! When are you leavin'?"

"Next week 'n' shit", Eric said.

"That soon?!" Eric nodded. "Dang, dude! Well, we're gonna hafta cruise South Main tonight and check out the Santa Cruz boardwalk 'n' shit tomorrow. Maybe some other shit before you leave."

"I was hopin' you'd say that, man."

We called up Jay and asked him if he wanted to come along on tonight's cruise. He said, "Sure, I'll go. I'll meet you guys at Eric's after I get off work 'n' shit."

Told you we used "'n' shit" a lot. We used it so much that some folks mocked us for it; as if we cared...'n' shit.

"Ok. See you then."

We also called Smurf who said he's in and would meet us at Eric's later that evening.

So Eric and I had some time to kill before everyone met up at his place. Eric was the youngest guy in our group at about 17. He, Jay and Brett smoked and Eric liked keeping his room dimly lit with the drapes drawn closed all the time. He put aluminum foil on the inside of the glass diffuser on the overhead light fixture to greatly diminish the amount of light it produced. His dad was also a smoker so the entire house had a perpetual haze which lingered in the air. His parents were rational people and, realizing how irrational it would be for them to lecture Eric on how bad it was to smoke, they chose to enable him, as long as he got his cigarettes from them rather than strangers. They also shared my own mother's philosophy about underage drinking. They knew that Eric would start drinking way before he turned 21 so, rather than have him out who knows where drinking who knows what with folks they haven't met, they enabled him to enjoy beer at home.

I looked over at Eric and asked, "Hey, man, what say we head over to Noah's? Maybe check out the arcade on Cannery Row 'n' shit?"

"Fer sure, dude. Just let me put out this cigarette and we'll split", he said as he got up from his chair and mashed what was left of his Marlboro into his ashtray on the nightstand.

We stepped out of his room into the hallway then the living room out the front door of his house, strolled over to the Night Machine, hopped in, then headed off post. The drive to Noah's gave us an opportunity to get caught up.

"I'm livin' in the grad dorms at UCLA now. The differences between there and where I was last year are I'm much closer to the Chemistry building and the residents are allowed to drink alcohol 'n' shit. In fact, once each quarter, they have a dorm sponsored kegger."

"Oh man. Sounds like hella fun."

"Yeah it does, but it's not all fun and games. There's lots of class work, homework, lab work, studying, paper writing, 'n' shit... Besides, the grad dorms are populated by grad students. These guys are way more serious than the undergrads when it comes to their academic careers."

"Yeah, but you can drink all you want 'n' shit."

"Technically, I could, but first off, I don't have the money to keep me stocked in booze and second, I actually need to stay sober to finish school and get my degree. But, unlike last year, I don't hafta keep my micro-bar 'n' shit hidden."

My micro-bar was a milk crate on its side that started out with gin, rum, vodka, and tequila in it sitting atop a small refrigerator wherein I made ice-cubes and kept mixers. In the undergrad dorms, I had to keep it covered with a towel to perpetuate the absurd illusion that there was no drinking in the dorms. Alright, to be fair, the on campus housing administration didn't condone, authorize or sanction the consumption of alcohol within the housing system and UCLA was a "dry" campus, but they knew they couldn't stop students from doing it. So, as long as you were reasonably discreet and didn't cause problems or become a spectacle, they tended to look the other way. In the grad dorms, I didn't have to keep my bar covered. Now because the undergrad students knew I had booze and dorm life was very inclusive, many of my dorm mates would stop by for a quick drink. This quickly got rather expensive for a student with limited resources. I noticed that everything but the gin would get drank up. When visitors would stop by and I welcomed them in with, "Would you care for a drink?", they would of course ask, "Whaddya have?"

When I answered, "Gin", they sounded disappointed in their response, "Oh. No thanks."

This was more than okay for me. I had developed a taste for gin long before I started at UCLA. By keeping only gin in my micro-bar, I could still be a cordial host by offering to fix a drink while at the same time not go broke supporting everyone else's drinking habit.

* * *

Anyway, Noah lived with his parents on Trapani Circle in Monterey. We had to meander our way through Fort Ord to the main gate then take Hwy. 1 south to Hwy. 68, also known as the Monterey Salinas Highway. Coming off the 68, we went up Josselyn Canyon Rd. which took us into Noah's neighborhood. As we came around the corner, we could see his '67 Camaro in the driveway which let me know he was home. I parked my Night Machine adjacent to the driveway, Eric and I stepped out of the car then went down the driveway, along the right side of the garage, then into the backyard. Noah's room, which he shared with his brother Adam — can you see a biblical theme here? — was a really nicely done converted garage with its own entrance facing the backyard. This allowed Noah to come and go, and receive visitors without them going through his parents' house. We knocked on his door then heard, "Come on in, guys!"

"Yo, man. How's it hangin'?"

"A little to the left, dude. Welcome back."

"Thanks, it's good to be back. Lookin' forward to hangin' with everyone, enjoyin' the time away from school 'n' shit."

"How's your second year goin' so far?"

"Cool, man, haven't blown up the chem lab yet…"

After a few minutes of chitchat, we clued him in on that night's cruise, "We're gonna meet at Eric's place. Interested?"

"I'd really like to but my parents already roped me into this thing they're havin' here at the house and expect all us kids to be there 'n' shit."

Noah had two more siblings in addition to Adam; I think they were named Gabriel and Martha — more biblical names.

I said, "That's a drag, dude, but no sweat." I then asked, "Hey, wanna come with us to Cannery Row for a little bit? Maybe troll for chicks? Then maybe check out some albums 'n' shit at Recycled Records?"

"Yeah, man. Let's go."

"Should I drive the Night Machine or do you wanna take your *'Stang*?"

Though Noah only had a Camaro, we never understood why he would occasionally get "nice 'Stang" compliments in reference to his car; 'Stang is short for Mustang. Go figure.

Noah turned his head toward us slightly and, with a subtle grin, emphatically responded, "The *Camaro*."

I rode shotgun and Eric had the backseat all to himself. Hitting the record shop and the arcade at Cannery Row were among the myriad of activities we did to pass the time. The arcade had an antique carousel in it which is now long gone but Recycled Records still exists. The afternoon was waning so we headed back to Noah's where Eric and I got in the Night Machine and went back to Fort Ord. I dropped

Eric off at his house then went home for some chow and to get ready for tonight, Friday night.

* * *

Before I go on, I should mention that the cruising scene in Salinas was like most street cruises in cities and towns throughout the country. There were lots of cars, many customized or modified, filled with young hormonal dudes and chicks out on the town looking to have a good time. The dudes were showing off their cars and girlfriends, and the chicks were showing off their scantily clad bodies. It was serendipitous that Salinas High School was very close to the north end of South Main. Many of the cruisers were, after all, high school students and recent grads. Most of the cars were driving up and down South Main with many parked in lots belonging to businesses which had closed earlier in the day. Since South Main is two-lanes each way and it was very congested during cruising hours, you could slowly cruise right up alongside another car and briefly chat. I remember seeing only a couple of fist fights; in one of them, the aggressor had thrown his opponent up against the side of my car as I was cruising by. "HEY!", I yelled, "Watch the paint!" Good times.

There's an unspoken understanding that you never cruise alone. We looked upon lone cruisers as weird and/or creepy. Everyone knows this is where all the cool kids come to cruise, meet people, and hang out. The only times I cruised alone was when I was on my way to pick up a friend, right after I dropped him off, or I was meeting someone on South Main. During one of those very rare occasions where I cruised alone there was one time where I had a very strong suspicion that my car would be stolen or I would get rolled, or both.

At the southern end of South Main, I pulled into a gas station which was closed for the night, i.e., all lights turned off, on a corner with two driveways in order to turn around and cruise back the other way one final time for the night. There were about a dozen cars parked in the darkness at this gas station. As I slowly pulled in, some guys approached my car, one on each side and two in front, compelling me to stop. My headlights revealed most of the parked cars to be nice looking lowriders. The guy on the driver's side said, "Hey, man, can you give me a jump?" Meanwhile, the guy on the passenger's side peered his head through my passenger window and was looking around as though he was shopping, kinda sizing up the condition of my car's interior. To say I was spooked is an understatement.

Keeping my cool, I said, "Sorry, man, I don't have any cables", which was a lie; any gearhead worth their weight in salt always has jumper cables and a toolbox with tools in case of a breakdown.

"No problem", he said, "we got cables."

Red flags and skyrockets went up in my brain loudly broadcasting that this was a setup. All the while, the guy on the passenger side continued checking out my car, even looking down at the front and rear wheels, and the two guys in front were just casually standing there, blocking my path. Some other guys were lurking in the shadows just beyond the beams of my headlights. I asked myself, 'if they have jumper cables, how could there be a dozen cars and not one single one of them is running so as to give this one guy a jump?' I had to quickly think up a way out of this situation before it escalated into an incident. If I could just get to the other driveway off to my right, I could leave and I'd be home free.

"Which car is it", I asked.

Pointing at the car to my immediate left, he said, "This one right here."

"Ok. What side's the battery on", I asked.

"The driver's side", he replied.

"Ok. Since my battery's on the passenger side, I'll need to pull in and turn around in order to line it up."

When I said that, the look on their faces left absolutely no doubt. They had just realized a major flaw in the execution of their plan. They needed to get me out of my car in order to steal it without much fuss. If they tried to force their plan at this stage with me behind the wheel and the car still in gear, they knew all I would have to do is hit the accelerator and I'd be gone in a flash. They were committed to their story and couldn't change it without giving themselves away and they were hoping I was still ignorant enough to let them do it.

"Oh", the guy said upon realizing his error. "Ok, so, are you gonna help me jump my car?"

"Sure, man", I answered in an upbeat tone, "I just need some space to turn around."

"Are you sure? You really gonna jump me", he asked again.

"Yes. As soon as I can get turned around. I just need to pull in that way", gesturing to my 2-o'clock — the direction of the other driveway —, "then back up that way", pointing in front of me, "so that I can line up the front of my car up to the front of your car."

"Oh. Ok. So, you sure you're gonna jump me?"

"Yeah, man, I'm sure."

With that, the guys flanking me stepped away and the guys in front parted like the Red Sea. I then pulled in as I said I would and calmly continued through the small lot out the other driveway, back onto South Main then straight home, never looking back. I didn't even bother to make that final pass down the street.

Yeah, cruising South Main had some rare unsavory moments but for the most part, there weren't any problems.

* * *

Like I was saying before I went off on that long ass tangent, on that December 11th evening, I went over to Eric's to hang out and wait for Jay and Smurf. Because Eric and his father were getting ready to move to Kansas, their place was looking kinda Spartan; a stark reminder of the transitory nature of military families. The drapes in Eric's window were gone as were all his posters and wall decorations but the foil was still in the overhead light fixture. His stereo had been packed up and he only had a boom box on which to play music. I came to the door of his house and knocked on it.

I heard Eric yell, "Come on in, Mark!"

I went into his room and closed the door. He had a lit cigarette in the ashtray. I asked, "Anyone else going with us tonight?"

"I called Martin but there was no answer."

"So it's just you, me, Smurf, and Jay?"

He answered, "Mm hmm" while taking a drag off his cigarette. He then put one of his favorite tapes in the boom box, Slayer's *Reign in Blood* which he called 'Region of Blood', sat back in his chair and blew smoke rings. I sat in a chair next to his bed.

Eric confided in me, "Man, I really don't wanna to go to Kansas. I'd rather stay here in California but I don't know where I'd live."

"I know whatcha mean, dude. In a perfect world, we'd be independently wealthy and have a big ol' mansion with a huge-ass garage for our cars 'n' shit, and just hang out, cruise around, pick up chicks, and party down", a la *Rock and Roll All Nite* by KISS.

Eric went on, "Me 'n' Jay have been playin' the Lotto 'n' shit. If we win, we'll do just that."

Smurf came by at around quarter after seven. While we were waiting for Jay, we hung out in Eric's room, shot the shit, listened to music, and snacked on some chips and soda.

It was just before 8:00 o'clock in the evening when we heard footsteps coming down the hallway. The door opened and there stood a shadowy figure backlit against the bright lights in the hallway streaming through the cigarette smoke; it was Jay. As he stepped into the darkened room, closing the door behind him, his features became visible in the dim light emanating from the muted overhead light. Standing about 5' 10" tall, he looked very much like a surfer with light blond hair and an athletic physique. He was usually clean shaven but his facial hair was also light blond so you couldn't tell if he hadn't shaven unless you were up close. He wore jeans, sneakers, and an unbuttoned flannel shirt over a T-shirt. He showed up having come straight from work. Since he pretty much lived at Eric's place, he came and went unannounced. He carried himself with an air of rebellious self-made independence which others found romantic and admirable. This attracted the likes of Smurf and Eric who saw him as a role model.

"Hey, Mark, glad you're back from college 'n' shit," he said retrieving a pack of cigarettes from his shirt pocket then pulling one from the pack.

"Me too, dude. I've been gettin' that a lot today," referring to the "...back from college..." comment. "How's the cosmos been treatin' you 'n' shit?" I asked as he lit his cigarette using the Zippo Eric kept on the nightstand.

Taking a long drag then exhaling the smoke, he casually answered, "Same ol' fuckin' bullshit."

He plopped himself on Eric's bed. Despite the odor of cigarettes in the room, I caught a whiff of pizza when he did that; Jay worked at a pizza parlor. I could tell there was something more going on than him just shaking off the drudgery from the day's work, but I wouldn't know what it was for another week.

"Eric tells me you've been stayin' here a lot."

"Yeah I have," he answered.

In a nonchalant tone, he went on, "My parents have been real dicks lately so I've been stayin' here 'n' shit."

"I know whatcha mean, dude, it sucks when parents act like dicks."

I didn't know at that time just how much it really *did* suck for Jay. He wasn't one to open up about that kind of stuff and I wasn't one to pry. He then asked, "So, we ready to go?"

Just a few moments later, we were all in the Night Machine ready to make our way to Salinas. Jay rode shotgun while Eric and Smurf were in the backseat. We left Eric's military housing area and turned onto Imjin Parkway, out Fort Ord's back gate, right turn onto Reservation Road, then left onto Blanco Road; next stop, Salinas. Every time we headed out to go cruising, excitement was in the air. Opportunities and adventure were waiting for us, anything could happen and it usually did. I can almost hear the Loverboy song, *Working for the Weekend*.

The drive along Blanco Road to Salinas that night gave us a little time to get caught up and reminisce about past escapades during previous cruises.

Eric declared, "Man Mark, I'm so glad you're back from college. Cruisin' South Main just ain't the same without you 'n' shit. Remember that time when that chick came out of her car, crossed the street, and handed you a note with her number on it? Then after we turned around you stuck your hand out the window with a note for her? That was funny as shit how she almost fell down when she came runnin' across the street to get the note. Or, how 'bout that time when those dudes saw your long hair and thought you were a chick until they saw your face and then one of them said to his buddy, 'Ooo! Tried to scam on a dude!'?"

"Yeah. That's when I decided to really let my moustache grow out."

One time when it was Brett, Eric and me, and we were on our way home from South Main, we crashed a house party we just happened to stumble upon.

Those folks had been partying for some hours and didn't care that we just "showed up" out of nowhere.

"Hey, I wonder if we'll see that dude with the blue metal-flake Trans Am", I remarked. "That's totally the most bad-ass metal-flake paint job I've ever seen."

I think it was Smurf who asked, "You know that dude, right?"

"Yeah I do. He was in my automatic transmission class at MPC. He did that paint himself."

"You ever gonna paint the Night Machine like that?"

"Are you kidding? Aside from the amount of time and work a paint job like that takes, I'd be forever paranoid that it would get all fucked up 'n' shit like in a parkin' lot or somethin'. Besides, the last time I painted my car, the neighbors called the fire department reporting that a gas leak was comin' from our house."

I had painted my Night Machine shortly after the Bhopal gas leak disaster of 1984 so the whole world was hypersensitive to any sort of chemical odor potentially being a deadly gas leak.

I went on, "My mom's still pissed about that."

Jay usually participated in the conversation but that night, he didn't really say much which meant that there was something on his mind; he was pondering what he was going to do once Eric and his dad Rick leave. In other words, he was trying to figure out who all else he could couch surf with so as to avoid going home to his dysfunctional parents. You see, because Jay was a bit rough around the edges he didn't have a lot of friends. Moreover, very few of those friends, that is to say their parents, would let him stay the night. Jay stoically kept all this to himself but I could tell it was weighing on him. What I couldn't tell was that this was a harbinger.

From Blanco road, we made a left turn directly onto South Main and started cruising. We always started from the southern end heading north and we were almost always in the left lane. That allowed us to easily see the cars coming from the opposite direction, and casually check out the cars to our right. On the northern end, we would make a left on Clay St. then, just passed Clay's Liquor, another left onto Lincoln Ave. which would bend left at Seaside High after a couple of blocks, becoming Chestnut St. which emptied out onto South Main where we turned right to go south. The turnaround point on the southern end was normally at San Joaquin St. This night of cruising was no more or less remarkable or memorable than most any other night. We had lots of fun and stayed out late.

Although I knew I was going to be home for only three weeks, it felt really good nonetheless. Little did I know that this was sort of like the calm before the storm that was set to hit next weekend.

Hey Man, I
Need Your Help

I took Eric up to the Santa Cruz beach boardwalk the next day. On the way back we stopped off at the Northridge Mall to play some games at their arcade. A couple days later, we bid Eric farewell. Jay had a job so he couldn't come out and play until after work whereas Noah didn't work, so, he and I had lots of time to hang out and do stuff during the day.

On the night of Friday, the 18th, Noah and I went to Mother's in San Jose. He was always a bit shy with the ladies and I had been helping him overcome it. I figured by going to Mother's, being that it was far enough from Monterey that nobody would know who we were, if either of us were to embarrass ourselves, none of our other friends would ever find out. So, I noticed how he was eyeing a few of the chicks there whereupon I said, "Go ask one of them to dance."

"Nah, man. They'll probably turn me down."

"So what, it's not like you're askin' for their hand in marriage 'n' shit. Besides, you won't know unless you ask."

Throughout the evening, I'd been keeping an eye on this one cute chick who kept turning down one guy after another. I then pointed her out to Noah and said to him, "See that ice princess right there? She's been wavin' off every dude that's asked her to dance. Look..."

Just then, yet another hopeful shmuck asked her to dance and was summarily shooed away like a pesky fly. I figured, as an example for Noah to show him it's no big deal to be turned down, I'd ask her to dance so he could watch me get waved away like all the others.

"It's no big deal gettin' turned down 'n' shit. Here, watch this", I said.

I went up to her and asked, "Pardon me, but would you care to dance?"

She smiled and said, "Sure."

I don't know who was more shocked, me or Noah. Talk about conflicting feelings. On the one hand, here I was, my buddy's wingman, totally expecting to be shot down in flames by this complete babe, ready to "take a bullet", so to speak, for my pal, when, out of all the dudes who asked her, she said "yes" to me. On the other hand, I was thinking to myself, 'Dude! This *totally hot babe* wants to dance with *me*.'

Well, as you can imagine, after we were done dancing and I went up to Noah, he gave me this priceless look that was like a combination of being pissed, embarrassed, and disbelief. The first thing I said to him was, "Dude! I *totally* expected her to say 'no'!"

His expression didn't change.

"I mean, you *saw* her turn down every other guy who asked her to dance 'n' shit!"

Still no change.

"It's not like I could tell her, 'just kidding, I'm tryin' to make a point'. I had to do the gentlemanly thing and follow through."

"Yeah, right, and I bet she *begged* you to take her phone number too", he finally said.

For the record, I didn't get her number. I simply smiled and thanked her. Yet, I still felt really bad for Noah. Especially now after that spectacle. So, I did what any self-respecting dedicated wingman would do in that situation; I made it my mission to get a chick to dance with him. I noticed that of all the chicks he glanced at that evening, there was one whom he seemed particularly smitten with. As a distraction, I sent Noah to the bar to get us a couple of drinks — remember, this was a 16-21 place so they only served soft drinks, no alcohol — then I headed straight for that chick and introduced myself.

"Hi, my name is Mark."

"Hi Mark, I'm Kelly, pleased to meet you."

"So, are you local to San Jose?"

"I live in Sunnyvale, and you?"

"My friend and I came up from Monterey." I then pointed him out and said, "He's over at the bar getting some drinks."

"Monterey? That's a bit of a ways."

"Yeah it is, but the scene here is *way* better 'n' shit."

As we continued to talk, I could tell she was totally down to earth so I talked up Noah to her. "My buddy's name is Noah, like with guy with the ark. He's kinda bashful and has been wanting to ask you to dance all night but can't muster the courage."

"He's kinda cute and I like bashful. I'd totally dance with him."

It would've been kismet if just then the DJ were playing *He's So Shy* by the Pointer Sisters.

"Oh, that's great. I'll send him right over."

I could also tell she had a really good sense of humor so I leaned a bit closer to her and said, "By the way, he'd be *totally* embarrassed if he knew I told you this but, rumor has it that he sometimes puts out on the first date. Don't' tell anyone, though."

We both smiled and giggled about that. I went over to Noah and said to him, "Hey, man, that chick you've been checkin' out all night wants to dance with you. You best go over there and ask her out onto the dancefloor right **now**. If you don't, you'll *never* hear the end of it from me."

He went over to her, she then took him by the hand, and they made their way onto the dancefloor; mission accomplished. Now I could see about getting to know that chick who unexpectedly agreed to dance with me, but alas, she was nowhere to be found. Que sera. Plenty of other chicks to dance with.

Noah and I stayed there until they closed; around 1:00 or 2:00 o'clock in the morning. Then on the way home, I asked him, "Did you have a good time 'n' shit?"

"Yeah I did. Got her number and everything. By the way, what did you say to her?"

"Nothin' but the truth — that you'd put out on the first date."

We laughed.

Noah was more liberal with his emotions than most guys. Though he did his best to hide it, I could tell he let himself develop feelings for that chick. It would've been apropos if Boston's *More Than a Feeling* were playing on the radio just then.

"Wanna cruise South Main tomorrow night?"

"Of course."

* * *

It was kinda weird getting ready to cruise South Main without Eric. Jay, Smurf and Noah met at my place. Jay seemed to have a more foreboding air about him than he did last week. Nevertheless, we would be cruising in his car. He had just washed his bright red Firebird that afternoon and it was looking sharp. So, I rode shotgun and Noah and Smurf were in the backseat. Just like last Friday, we left Fort Ord out the back gate, right on Reservation Rd. then left onto Blanco. This time, I think the Saga song, *On the Loose* may have been playing on the radio. We turned onto the left lane of South Main heading north and after a couple of blocks, we were in the thick of the cruise. The Firebird was garnering attention form the chicks and green gazes from the dudes. In retrospect, we should've nicknamed his car the "Peacock".

I don't remember how long, or rather how briefly we had been cruising that night when, heading southbound on South Main, Jay had pulled into the left-turn only lane to go onto Pine Street across from Salinas High. I think it was around 10:00 or 11:00 o'clock at night. We were going to drive through the gas station on the corner to turn around to follow a car with some chicks in it that we were flirting with. While waiting behind one car for the light to change, Jay looked at his review mirror and calmly uttered, "Don't look, but, my dad's behind us."

Smurf and Noah, in the back seat, both turned to look.

I know, huh.

Really!?

Tension in the car instantly peaked. The only sounds heard were the street traffic and the music broadcasting over the radio. The tension was so great that I don't even remember what song was playing. Jay, still looking in his review mirror, broke the silence saying, "Oh shit. He knows he's in for a chase."

"How do you know?", I asked.

"He just put his seatbelt on."

* * *

There's a saying amongst motorcyclists that goes, "There are lots of old bikers and there are lots of bold bikers, but there aren't any old bold bikers." Unbeknownst to me at this moment in time, I was at the starting gate of the adventure of a lifetime and it was about to begin the way every James Bond movie starts; with an adrenalin pumping action sequence.

"A chase? Whaddya mean 'a chase'? Is he gonna follow us 'n' shit? Why would he do that?", I asked Jay.

"My dad's restricted my use of my car and now he probably wants to punish me for takin' it out without his permission."

There was something irrational about this that started me wondering. The clock was ticking … the light would soon turn green. There were dozens of questions swirling about in my mind, so many, in fact, that I couldn't decide on which one was most important to ask first. I had no concept of the dynamics of the situation until the light turned green. And when it did, the car in front of us, followed closely by Jay in his Firebird, started its left turn onto Pine. Just then, Jay's dad quickly veered inside the left turn to try to cut Jay off. Fortunately for us, a car coming up Pine had pulled into its left-turn lane thereby preventing Jay's dad from completing his maneuver.

'Fuuuuck', I thought to myself, 'Jay wasn't kidding'.

The car in front of us turned into the gas station then Jay mashed the accelerator and we were off, with his father in hot pursuit. I cannot remember what Noah and Smurf were yelling but it was noisy and distracting to Jay.

"Shut the hell up and let Jay focus!"

Jay did what he could to shake his dad making a quick right then left then right..., at one point, in order to avoid a car stopped in the street, he made an impromptu detour over someone's front yard, all the while his dad was right behind us. It all went so fast that I don't remember which streets we roared down in that sleepy bedroom community neighborhood. If any residents were witness to this exhibition, I can only imagine what they must have been thinking; "What the *fuck* are them damn kids doin' now!?"

"Mark! You gotta help me lose my dad!"

'How am I gonna do that', I wondered for a moment. Then it came to me and I asked him, "What kind of car is your dad drivin'?"

Jay told me but I can't recall the make, let alone the model, however I do remember it was a late model four-cylinder powered front-wheel drive. "Dude, that's a front-wheel drive car! You'll never be able to outrun him in a neighborhood makin' a bunch of turns 'n' shit! You need to get onto a straightaway where your V8 will leave his four-banger in the dust!"

Jay then went straight, coaxing everything he could out of the Firebird's V8, blowing through stop signs, only to be impeded by a car pulling out of a driveway. Daringly swerving around it, coming face to face with oncoming traffic, narrowly missing both by mere inches, he resumed his straight-line sprint. Jay's dad momentarily got delayed by the two cars then tried to resume his pursuit. I noticed the headlights of his car getting smaller with the passing of every second. Speedily approaching a T-intersection, Jay turned right and we slid through the red-light onto Abbott Street heading south toward Blanco.

"Make a left here on Blanco! This'll take you to the freeway!" I declared.

Blowing through another red-light, we slid onto Blanco, which becomes Sanborn at Abbott, heading north toward highway 101 at full-throttle. Looking out the rear window, I couldn't tell if Jay's dad was still following us or not; there were no headlights to be seen. Jay wasn't letting up, though. We sped over the bridge above the railroad tracks then under the 101, turning right onto Fairview to catch the northbound 101. This totally reminds me of *Red Barchetta* by Rush. Jay got on the freeway, went over the overpass, took the off-ramp that leads back onto Sanborn and stopped about half-way down the off-ramp, then cut his headlights. Now we waited. For what seemed like an hour — it was really only about ten-minutes —, we waited to see if Jay's father would appear. He didn't. We were in the clear... for now.

Jay was, indeed, a bold driver. There were at least a handful of moments where we were within a hair's breadth of disaster. Repurposing someone's lawn to be a bypass was bold. He also knew how to think fast on his feet and adapt to the situation at hand. When we got on the 101, I figured we'd race up to Northridge Mall so as to put as many miles between us and Jay's dad as possible, but Jay's decision to hideout in the shadows of the off-ramp was brilliant.

* * *

Smurf and Noah were understandably shaken. Not about nearly being killed or maimed in a horrific car wreck, but about getting in trouble with their parents. Ah, the priorities of unbridled youth.

Jay turned his headlights on and cautiously drove the rest of the way down the off-ramp back onto Sanborn.

As we were making our way back to Fort Ord, we said to Jay, "Duuude... what's up with your dad, man? He's gotta be all *totally* fuckin' pissed to chase us like that. Whatcha gonna do?"

"I don't know, man, but I'll hafta think of somethin'."

After a few minutes, to break the tension, I said, "Man, I can't believe you drove over that dude's lawn 'n' shit. Just imagine the next time he goes to mow it and he sees some big-ass ruts in it."

We all snickered about that then energetically rehashed the various highlights of the chase and subsequent getaway. We were a carload of adrenalin pumped firebrands who had been emboldened by the act of getting away from, and out smarting, a parental unit. However, we were still cautious. Jay didn't know where his dad went after suffering his humiliating defeat. For all we knew, he was at Smurf's house. That actually would've worked in our favor because Smurf lived clear on the other side of Fort Ord. Mind you, I didn't know Jay's dad much beyond an introduction and handshake, and, fortunately, he didn't know where I lived... or did he?

"Yo Jay, does your dad know where I live?"

"Nah, I doubt it", he replied.

"Well, suppose he did, think he'd be stakin' out my house 'n' shit?"

"No way, man. Even if he did know, he probably just drove by your house to see if my car was there. He absolutely wouldn't stick around 'n' shit."

We took a more surreptitious route back to my place. We took Reservation Rd. into Marina and made a left onto Del Monte Blvd. which empties onto Hwy. 1. We then took the first exit which was the Imjin Pkwy gate and meandered our way back to my place. Jay's dad's car was nowhere in sight so Noah, Smurf and I got out, bid Jay farewell, then parted ways.

As I went inside, I was thinking how messed up it was that Jay's dad had totally ruined our hunt for those hotties in that other car we wanted to follow.

* * *

The next day, a message from Jay was relayed to me by Smurf or Martin that he wanted to see me. He was at one of the nondescript "no-tell" motels along what we called "motel row" in Monterey where I went to meet with him.

"Hey, man, what's been goin' on", I asked. "What happened last night when you got home 'n' shit?"

"I didn't go home, I got a room here. Man, I'm *not* goin' back. I need to go to Indiana."

Jay often mentioned that he had family roots in Indiana and just as frequently expressed his desire to return there.

"I gotta go to Indiana, man. There's *no* way I can go back to my parents, my dad would totally fuckin' kill me 'n' shit. I wanted to talk to you to ask you if you can help me get to my grandma's place in Indiana."

Whoa. This guy's making a pretty big decision. Jay and I weren't close the way I was with Eric or how Eric was with him so it was a big step for him to take me into his confidence like this.

"Dude, for real?", I asked.

"For real."

"Ok. How 'bout you give me the reasoning behind your decision to move to Indiana."

Jay was all over the place and initially couldn't organize his thoughts. I helped him compartmentalize and focus on one facet at a time and derived therefrom the complete picture. I was seeing a side of Jay that I never knew existed. He was exposing his darkest secrets to me thus making himself completely vulnerable. He had always been very reserved and kept his feelings close to the vest which made me think he was shallow when quite the opposite was true. The only other guy he was this candid with was Eric.

As you likely suspected, Jay's home life was less than idyllic. I'm not saying that most folks grow up in a perfect nurturing environment, we've all had to endure varying degrees of dysfunctionality. It's just that Jay's home was more dysfunctional than most, as you'll see.

I'll spare you the graphic details Jay relayed to me about the physical abuses he and his sister endured but I will share that he emphasized that there was no sexual abuse. I'll just get right to the crux of the emotional torment.

With some financial help from his grandmother, Jay added money he got from her to money he had saved in order to purchase his Firebird at the age of 17. Being under 18, he couldn't register it in his name so it was registered in his father's name. The understanding was that Jay would be financially responsible for the car, i.e., working a job to pay for registration, insurance, gas, repairs, etc., and his parents would transfer the title and registration to Jay when he turned 18. Well, when he did, they didn't. On the contrary, Jay's parents used his car as a means of controlling him. They verbally abuse him, labeled him as lazy, stating that he couldn't keep a steady job, he'd never amount to anything... They told him to go out and get a job which he did. After some weeks, they would take his car keys away as punishment for some trivial offense, thus preventing him from being able to drive to work which also prevented him from taking Eric to work. Keep in mind, there were no jobs for high schoolers on the Army post, only on the local economy off-post. Fort Ord was a big place so to get to anywhere off-post, you had to drive.

Anyway, because Jay couldn't drive to work, he'd lose his job, whereupon his parents would call him lazy, etc., give him his keys back and send him out to get a job...rinse, repeat. The psychological and emotional toll that sort of treatment takes on a teenager is immeasurable. A fat lip or bruises will eventually heal leaving no marks but the mental injuries from this could last indefinitely.

Here was a brave, strong young man on the edge, reaching out to me asking if I would help him find salvation. He was in a situation that could go sideways so easily. After trusting me enough to confide in me the way that he did, how could I not help him? What kind of an example would I set for him and how could I live with myself if I just walked away?

"Alright, man", I said while *We're Not Gonna Take It* by Twisted Sister was playing in the background, "I'll help you. So, what's your plan?"

Jay had been mulling this over for quite some time and had formulated a rather solid foundation, it just needed some fine tuning and a few gaps filled in. He was going to first drive his Firebird to Fort Hood in Texas to visit his girlfriend Leanne, then, from there, go north to his grandmother's place in Indiana.

"How're you gonna pay for shit like gas 'n' food?"

"I was thinkin' about sneakin' into my parent's house and take one of their credit cards, and gather up my valuables 'n' shit to sell so we'd have some cash."

"We?"

"Yeah, man. I want you to come along as my mechanic in case my car breaks down", Jay answered.

"Dude... I'm on winter break from UCLA and need to be back in class on the morning of January 4th, and Christmas is this Friday! Let's say I go with you 'n' shit, you're on a one-way trip, how am I gonna get back in time for class?"

"My grandma's got money, she'll pay for your ticket back."

While he was pleading his case, I was thinking how appealing it would be to go on a whirlwind road trip during winter break and what sort of a cool story it would make compared to the rest of the students in the dorms. You know, some yuppie blowhard douchebag would boast, "We went skiing in Aspen Colorado. What did *you* do?"

To which I would counter, "Well, after a high-speed car chase in Salinas, we hauled ass across the country in a Firebird."

Yeah, that's right, whose story is cooler?

Anyway, after a little more pleading and convincing, I said, "Ok. You're obviously serious about doin' this. If you really want my help 'n' shit then you'll need to do everything I tell you to do without exception and without argument. It won't be easy because I know how you are, but that's the *only* way I'll agree to go all in. Can you do that?"

"Absolutely, man. Aw dude, thank you, *thank you*, **thank you**."

"Ok, rule number one: do what I tell you to do. The most important thing for you to do right now is *keep quiet*. You must NOT tell **anyone** what you're plannin', where you're goin', or even that you're leavin'. You can't say anything to Eric, Smurf, Noah, Leanne, your grandma... anyone. From what you told me about your parents, I would expect they will put extreme pressure on everyone they know who knows you to snitch on you and spill whatever they know 'n' shit. The simple fact remains that they can't talk about somethin' they themselves don't know about. So, you need to keep your mouth *shut*. Like they say, 'the only way for two guys to keep a secret is if one of them is dead.' Don't make me hafta kill ya dude."

"Totally, man. You got it."

"Alright, then. We've got work to do."

* * *

During my first quarter at UCLA, one of the friends I made was a very resourceful, very helpful,

47

very trustworthy young man named Mario with a very close, well connected family. He and I shared a number of exploits during that first quarter which I may tell you about some other time. To help Jay raise funds, I reached out to Mario for assistance. You see, the route Jay and I were going to drive took us down U.S. highway 101 to Los Angeles where we would catch interstate highway 10 to Texas. Los Angeles would be the ideal place to unload Jay's valuables. Going to someplace like a pawn shop in Monterey may raise suspicions and likely result is less cash. Selling items to one or more friends goes against rule number two: communication blackout.

After I left Jay at the motel, I went home to initiate contact with Mario, my operative in L.A., and arrange for a rendezvous; imagine the theme from *Mission Impossible* playing in the background. Meanwhile, Jay was preparing himself for a stealthy late-night operation with the mission objective being the retrieval of his stuff and the acquisition of a credit card from his parents. If all went well, Jay would pick me up from my place early the next morning.

* * *

My mother was in the Army and she was assigned family quarters on Fort Ord within a mile of Eric's place. Since Jay's parents never knew where I lived, my place could therefore be considered a type of safehouse.

I had to tell my mother I was going to be gone for a few days and I struggled with just how I was going to tell her that and what I was going to say. In the unlikely event that Jay's parents learned about my mother and questioned her about my whereabouts and whatnot, I didn't want for her to knowingly and actively engage in telling a lie in order to protect me and keep this mission secret. But, then again, my mother is not one to tell a lie. On the contrary, given the situation, I wouldn't have put it past her to take an assertive stance and insist that Jay stand his ground and reveal to the world the abusive conditions he and his sister were having to endure in their home. It wouldn't have been the first time my mother's helped abused children.

My mother's a very strong willed German born immigrant who grew up in post-WWII Germany during the reconstruction. Talk about tough as nails. She may only be 5'5", 120lb, but she's an insurmountable force to be reckoned with when riled up. Hence, I chose the path of least resistance.

I decided to reuse a lie I had used when I was a senior in high school so I could clandestinely fly from Puerto Rico to Germany to visit my then girlfriend — another story for another time. I told my mother I was going on a retreat. It was a believable lie that couldn't be challenged until the deed was done. The best lies are those rooted in facts; the more pieces of the lie that are factual and/or true, the more believable the lie becomes.

Earlier in my high school career while we were stationed at Fort Buchanan in Puerto Rico, one of my friends invited me to participate on a retreat. He neglected to tell me it was a religious retreat. Although it was fun for the most part, I could've done without all that bible preaching stuff; but, then again, that's the whole idea behind a religious retreat. Nevertheless, one of the unexpected benefits of the retreat was no communication with or interference from the outside world, save, of course, in the case of an emergency. This was the perfect cover story for why I'd be gone and wouldn't be able to call.

Back to the ruse I told my mom. I said that one of my friends invited me to a Christmas retreat and I would be gone for about a week. She was okay with that and wished me well. I packed my things and hit the sack early to get plenty of sleep.

* * *

Jay arrived early the next morning leading me to think his mission the night before was a success. When I debriefed him, I got confirmation. The credit card he lifted from his mom's wallet was a Discover card. How fortuitous! The significance associated with the Discover card is the company was just over a year old back then and it was not as widely accepted as its competitors American Express, Visa, Master Card, or even Diners Club. It just so happened I had a Discover card back then so I knew about this first hand.

"That's a brilliant choice," I said to him. "Of all the cards in your mom's wallet, why'd you choose the Discover card?"

"I just picked one of the ones in the back of the stack figurin' she wouldn't notice it right away."

Why over think it, right?

I told him, "I've got one of these too and not everyone'll take it. Your parents probably have the same experience and rarely, if ever, use it. There may be times where you'll hafta use cash, but as long as we can use the Discover card, we should be ok. I agree that they probably won't notice the card's missing until they get the bill 'n' shit."

"Cool. I also got my TV, camcorder...", and I can't remember the other items he had to hock. "I mean, the stuff's gotta be worth somethin', right? I paid good money for it when I bought it."

"Great. When we get to L.A., I know a guy who'll work with us to sell this stuff. We should hit the road immediately and just go straight through to L.A. 'n' shit. Every moment we delay is another moment your parents may discover us."

I put my bag in the trunk of the Firebird and tossed my jacket, a camouflage army field jacket with a removable thermal lining, in the backseat. I sat down in the passenger seat then closed the door. Since Jay was a smoker, every time I stepped into his car, my olfactories were assaulted by the characteristic stench of stale cigarette smoke. Despite it being a crisp morning, I rolled down the window.

* * *

Like the old Chinese proverb said, "A journey of a thousand miles begins with a single step." For us, that single step was on the gas pedal of Jay's bright red Firebird. Look out, L.A., here we come.

I suppose I could paint the picture for you of how our sojourn began by retracing the same route we took to go cruising South Main. A route that normally charged the air with excitement and anticipation, now it was heavy with anxiety and uncertainty. I couldn't help but contemplate the irony. Almost like a fore-shadowing. As we passed South Main then Abbott where Blanco becomes Sanborn, Jay and I relived the last moments of the chase from the night before. Approaching the 101 overpass and turning onto the southbound onramp, it felt as though we came full circle.

Well, no sense dwelling over the unknown. L.A. is just over 300 miles away; we had our shades on, music cranked — think *Born to be Wild* by Steppenwolf — and a full tank of gas. All there was to do now was sit back, relax, and enjoy the ride.

On the road again

I'm no stranger to road trips. My earliest recollection of traversing the highways and byways of this great nation was with my mother driving from L.A. to Lexington Kentucky and back in her 1958 Chevy Impala back in 1971 — yes, I'm that old. That experience, as well as the others that followed, may have contributed to my passion for pavement. When I was building, customizing, and outfitting my Night Machine, I replaced the cracked factory tinted windshield with an un-tinted windshield so as to see better at night and I installed auxiliary forward lighting; fog lights and driving lights. Fortunately, the cruise control worked great. My long-term goal was to take an extended vacation and drive the Night Machine all around the country... that 8,000+ mile journey is a story for another time.

* * *

It was a typical December morning in central California. The sun shining through the driver's side window painted Jay in silhouette, almost like he was a shadow of his former self, as he was piloting his cherished Firebird away from tyranny and in search of independence and dignity, kinda like a metaphor for his emancipation from his parents. After merging onto the 101, the urban landscape briefly gave way to suburbs then rural farm fields. Since it was December, all the crops had been harvested and the fields were bare. Behind us, Salinas was fading into the horizon, and unknown adventures were waiting for us ahead.

Over the years, I had been both a passenger and a driver on the drive between L.A. and Salinas so many times that I don't remember any details from this specific trip. We likely talked about all manner of subjects under the sun; cars, chicks, school, who and what we'll miss, our route, what to expect, what we hope to find or encounter... A lengthy road trip consists of about 90% driving with the other 10% being the actual cool stuff you remember. One of the realizations I've made since then is there was a complete lack of vineyards. The few cultivated fields we could see from the freeway grew produce such as fruits and vegetables. Every time I've driven that route since, I saw a couple of wineries appear, then a couple more. The last time I drove that route, I saw one winery after another, their vineyards blanketing hillside after hillside. Some of those crop fields Jay and I drove past have since been transformed into vineyards. The once virgin landscape of rolling hills covered with wild grasses waving in the breeze is no more. Yet another sight of nature's wonder that's lost forever.

* * *

Every urbanized area, be it a small town, mega-lopolis, and everything in-between, has its own road-way vibe, a sort of interconnected melody making up an intangible rhythm which the locals are tuned-in to, but frustrates visitors. This vibe is largely rooted in the intimate knowledge of the roads which the locals enjoy and disenfranchises visitors. Los Angeles, being the birthplace of car culture, has the added dynamic of an extensive freeway system intended to allow users to get from one part of the city to another quickly and easily but it's been overtaxed for nearly as long as it's existed. To put it another way, too much traffic, not enough bandwidth. Driving anywhere in L.A. is also very taxing on the driver.

My buddy, Mario, lived in Hacienda Heights, an area unsuitable for freeways. There was no quick or easy way to get there and as Jay and I were approaching L.A., I was thinking of the best route in order to bypass as much traffic as possible. In Thousand Oaks, we took the 23 to the 118, stayed on that road till it ended at the 210 whence we headed east to the 605, turning south thereon, then getting on the 60 east, we ultimately exited at Hacienda Blvd. That's how Ange-linos speak when talking about the freeway system. Jay had never been to L.A. before so this was all new to him. He frequently expressed his gratitude that I knew where I was going and that I was guiding him.

"Daang!" he exclaimed. "Did you see that fuckin' dude? He just crossed over two-lanes and cut those guys off to get to the exit 'n' shit. They almost wrecked."

"That's how they drive here, man", I said matter of factly, "You've gotta be vigilant and pay extra attention because lots of these idiots don't. See about gettin' into the right-lane when it's safe 'n' shit; you'll be transitioning onto the 210 east in a couple of miles."

"I'm thinkin' I shoulda had you drive."

"You're doin' fine, dude. Just don't stress out."

After a couple more freeway interchanges, Jay managed to acclimate to the L.A. way of driving without too much difficulty. We headed south on Hacienda Blvd. once we exited the 60. Beyond Colima Road, the wide boulevard reduces down to a single lane winding road.

Coming up on a really sharp hairpin turn, I warned Jay, "There's a right-hand turn coming up where they're *really* not kidding about the reduced speed limit; I suggest you slow down 'n' shit."

He slowed down but was still going almost too fast for this turn, slid across the opposite lane and nearly into the hillside; fortunately, there was no oncoming traffic at that moment.

"Whoa! Shit, dude! That was close", he said.

"Dude! Remember rule number one?!"

"Sorry, man. I'm just anxious to get there."

"So am I, dude. Not only do I wanna get there quickly, I wanna make it there in one piece. You agreed to rule number one and you should know that it's not like I'm a backseat driver or I'm talkin' out the side of my neck. I'm not one to nag you that you're goin' too slow or too fast 'n' shit, but in the scenario like we just had where I've been on this road and I know its quirks, I *will* speak up and I expect you to think of me as E. F. Hutton."

For those of you who don't know or can't remember, E. F. Hutton is an investment firm whose slogan is, "When E. F. Hutton talks, people listen."

"You're right, man. I really am sorry." I knew he was sincere by the tone of his voice.

A couple miles further on, we pulled into Mario's driveway. The first leg of our journey now behind us, Mario greeted us, lavished hospitality upon us, and welcomed us into his home.

"Mario, this is Jay."

"Hi Jay, pleased to meet you, come on in, I've got some drinks and snacks for you guys. How was the drive?", he asked.

"Thanks, man", I responded. "Other than the usual idiot here and there who can't seem to tell the difference between a brake pedal and gas pedal, or can't figure out how to work the blinker 'n' shit, the drive was uneventful. Mind if we get right down to business?"

"Way ahead of you my friend. My brothers expressed interest in Jay's stuff. After you've taken the time to relax and freshen up, we'll go have a look."

The other day when I had called Mario about this, I explained the nature of the situation with the understanding of keeping it confidential. It just so happened that his brothers are lawyers and indicated that they would avail themselves should Jay or I need legal help.

After about an hour or so, Mario, Jay and I collected the items from Jay's car so Mario could look them over. He called his brothers on the phone and gave them a detailed inventory. It was decided that everyone meet at the home of the oldest brother, Oscar, since it was closer to Mario's place. I cannot for the life of me remember the name of the younger brother; they say memory is the first thing to go when you... dang it, how did that saying go?

Jay and I got into Mario's Nissan Sentra — Mario wasn't a gearhead — with Jay's things and went to Oscar's place.

Upon our arrival, we were warmly greeted and offered refreshments.

"Hi Mark, good to see you again. And you must be Jay."

Shaking hands, Jay smiled and answered, "Yes sir, hello."

Mario's family are all wonderful people who genuinely exude that "mi casa, su casa" feeling. So, after some time, Mario's brothers and their wives looked over Jay's things. Once again, unfortunately, the details of this transaction have faded from memory but the upshot was they gave Jay an amount that was about equal to market value.

Mario whispered in my ear, "Hope that's enough to get you guys to Indiana."

I whispered back, "I think it'll be fine, bro. Can't thank you and your brother's enough for this."

"Hey, man, it's Christmas time, you're part of the family and we gotta stick together and help each other out. Anytime you need something, you can always count on me."

Oscar announced, "Hey everyone! It's time to eat! Let's all go inside, we've got lots of tamales that need to be eaten!"

I failed to mention that Mario's mother owned and operated a Mexican restaurant. Jay was about to experience his first genuine authentic Mexican feast. Good thing we were hungry. I didn't know it then but Jay wasn't much into Mexican cuisine.

* * *

I barely managed to finish my third plateful of food when someone in Mario's family announced, "There're still more tamales for you to eat! Don't tell me you guys are full already."

Leaning as far back in the chair as I could while trying to take a deep breath followed by a strained sigh, I responded, "I feel like Mr. Creosote from Monte Python; if I have another bite, I'll explode."

Good thing Mario was driving. Many thank-yous, salutations and well-wishes were exchanged as we readied ourselves to go back to Mario's place where we were going to spend the night. Given how much we ate, we quickly fell into a food-coma when we hit the sack.

* * *

That next morning, we strived to get an early start. Jay was really eager to be with Leanne whom he hadn't seen in months and wanted to drive straight through to Fort Hood, located near Killeen, Texas, about 50 miles north of Austin, which is just over 1350 miles from L.A. Mario's mom made us chilaquiles for breakfast. That's when I noticed that Jay really was a Midwestern kinda guy; meat and potatoes. He ate the ham and eggs, but only nibbled on some of the corn tortillas, mostly pushing them around on his plate. He tried hard not to appear ungrateful or impolite. Fortunately, Mario's mom was very understanding and made something else for Jay. I, on the other hand, adore chilaquiles. In fact, the way I rate a Mexican restaurant I haven't been to before is by trying their chilaquiles. There are about as many different ways of preparing chilaquiles as there are Mexican restaurants. Each one reflects the pride taken by the cook in preparing it.

We thanked both Mario and his mom for their hospitality, packed up our things, and hit the road. We topped off the gas tank, got some maps, extra motor oil, transmission fluid, and coolant, went back the way we came down Hacienda Blvd. to get on highway 60 then headed east. So far, the Discover card was working which led me to think that Jay's parents hadn't noticed yet that it was gone. I'd like to think Boston's *Don't Look Back* was playing on the radio.

Jay was driving and I was navigating. The 60 ended around Beaumont California whence we merged onto interstate 10 and continued east.

"According to the map, we can stay on the 10 until somewhere in the middle of Texas before we hafta get on a different road 'n' shit. So, just keep goin' straight for about a thousand miles and make a left turn at Albuquerque", a reference to the Warner Bros. character Bugs Bunny. "Just kidding... about the Albuquerque part, that is, not about the 'thousand miles'."

Once we cleared Beaumont, there wasn't much to see. We were beginning our long journey across the sparsely populated expanse known as the great southwestern desert. Palm Springs was indicated by a sign pointing at an off-ramp. Back then there were only a handful of wind generators in that Palm Springs/Palm Desert corridor to break up the monotonous landscape along the interstate. Those generators represented an experimental pilot program which has since expanded into an enormous enterprise with hundreds of acres covered with wind generators

On crossing the border into Arizona, we started seeing signs for "The Thing". Roadside attractions were all the rage back in the day. I told Jay, "Back when I was a kid and my mom & I came this way, they used to have Indian tepees along the side of the road to attract passersby to their souvenir shops 'n' shit."

We didn't see any tepees. The previous times I traveled along this route, I noticed there were fewer and fewer tepees on each successive trip; perhaps the last remaining tepees were taken down by the time Jay and I drove through. We did, however, stop off at a Waffle House for some eats. We also fueled up the Firebird and went to a K-mart to do some shopping; Jay wanted to get some fog-lights for the Firebird and have me install them. Good thing it was winter otherwise I would've been really uncomfortable while doing that work in the parking lot.

Later on, we actually did go see "The Thing". It was only a dollar and we knew it would be corny. Hey, when you're on the road for hours at a time, it's worth a buck just to see something other than another boulder, more sand, a rest-stop, or a gas station.

The sun was setting and I was kinda looking forward to driving through the desert at night. For me, seeing nothing but bleak desert for hours on end during the day is more fatiguing than at night where all you can see are lights off in the distance and whatever your headlights illuminate directly in front of you. But, to each his own.

I mentioned earlier how Jay was most certainly a bold driver. He also liked to go fast; I suppose that kinda goes hand in hand. Imagine Sammy Hagar's *I Can't Drive 55* playing in the background as I tell you this. Anyway, it was not uncommon for Jay to be doing about a hundred miles an hour on the interstate when there didn't seem to be any other cars around; don't want to get popped by the cops. Driving fast at night was a bit of a double-edged sword. You can see another car from far away by its headlights. However, you wouldn't have time to react should something be in the road. Being that we were young firebrands, we lacked the prudence and reserve that wisdom, earned from experience, imparts. We were too impetuous to consider the risks of driving fast at night and Jay was too impatient. All that aside, we made some really good time. Even though the national speed limit was 55 mph, Jay soon became accustomed to doing between 100-120 mph along the interstate. On those occasional instances where Jay would have me drive so he could rest, I found myself rubbing elbows with the 100+ mph club as well. I was used to that in my Night Machine so this was old hat for me.

* * *

Some thirty miles or so before Las Cruces, New Mexico, at about 9:00 or 10:00 o'clock at night, we started seeing wisps of what appeared to be fog. I thought this was really odd because there were no bodies of water within several miles. 'Where could this fog be coming from?', I wondered. I even shared my bewilderment with Jay.

A few minutes later, we saw a car pulled over onto the shoulder with smoke billowing out from the engine compartment. Jay slowed down and as we passed, I saw the silhouette of a person slumped over the steering wheel.

"Jay! It looks like there's a dude in that car who might be dead or somethin'."

He replied, "We better see if he needs help."

Jay pulled over then backed up to the other car to see if there was a problem. An older dude stepped out of the car, smiling and said, "Thank you so much for stoppin'!"

"Are you alright? What's the problem?", I asked.

"My car started overheatin' and stopped runnin' so I pulled over, then all this smoke came out. I didn't know what I was gonna do. Thank the Lord you fellas stopped."

I asked him, "Do you have any clue what the problem may be?"

"No clue whatsoever. Would it be too much to ask you for a lift to Las Cruces?"

It was just a couple days before Christmas and pretty cold outside. I turned to Jay and said, "Well? I'm your mechanic. If you want, I can take a look at his car and if it's not too serious, I may be able to get him back on the road 'n' shit. Otherwise you'll need to decide if you wanna give him a ride into Las Cruces."

"Hey, man, if you wanna try and fix it, go ahead."

Turning back to the stranded motorist, I asked, "Mind if I take a look at your car, maybe see what the problem could be?"

"Oh goodness, if you would, that would be very nice of you."

The man had a comparatively late model car which aren't my forte but I figured that since the car was already broken, the worst that could happen is I can't fix it. I ultimately determined that one of the hose fittings on his heater core had broken off; it was made of plastic. I rolled my eyes when I discovered this; 'Damn modern cars using parts made of plastic, no wonder it broke off', I thought to myself. This totally made sense. It probably gave out some miles up the road. The hot liquid in the cold night air created the "fog" which Jay and I saw.

"Well, I think I found your problem", which I explained to him. "There's no way I can fix your broken heater core but I can bypass it thereby gettin' you back on the road provided nothin' else is wrong. You should be aware that you won't have any heat in your car."

"At this point, I could care less about havin' heat as long as you can get it runnin'."

I updated Jay that I could get him on the road but we'd need to use the extra coolant we had with us. He gave the OK so I got the tools out of Jay's car, went ahead and got the guy's car patched up, then filled up his radiator.

"Go ahead and start it", I said crossing my fingers hoping that there wasn't anything else wrong with his car.

The motorist started his car and was thrilled that it was running.

"Now hold on," I cautioned. "Let's give it some time to run and make sure you don't have any other coolant leaks. Watch your temperature gauge and let me know if it starts actin' weird 'n' shit."

"Whaddya mean by 'weird'?"

I decided to take a look at his instrument panel. It was all idiot lights, no gauges. "Never mind. Just keep it runnin' for now."

I kept checking the hoses for firmness and felt round the radiator for heat distribution. After about ten minutes, everything was still looking good and I said, "Well, looks like you're good to go. It should hold together long enough for you to replace your heater core."

He thanked us again, even gave us some money for the coolant. I packed up the tools as Jay tried to start his car. No go. Jay had left the lights on and the battery had drained to where it couldn't start the car. I went back to the motorist who fortunately hadn't left yet and asked, "Would you mind returnin' the favor?"

I got the jumper cables out of the Firebird, hooked the cars together, Jay started his car and we were back on the road. I guess that whole event could be chalked up as Christmas miracle, good karma, quid pro quo, etc., all rolled into one.

Back on the highway, Jay commented, "That was cool how you just fixed that dude's car right there on the spot 'n' shit. I'm glad you were able to get him back on the road."

Once again, Jay surprised me by displaying a compassionate side I didn't know he had.

"Well," I responded, "let's hope I *don't* hafta do that for *you*."

Seeing the lights of Las Cruces ahead of us in the distance, I said to Jay, "We could stop in Las Cruces for some gas and get some more coolant or we could continue on to El Paso. Either's fine."

"We still got about a half a tank 'n' shit", he replied.

"Alright. El Paso it is."

Deep in the Heart of Texas

Jay's Firebird wasn't the only thing that got fueled up in El Paso. He and I grabbed some eats to chow down on while on the road. We got back on interstate 10 and continued our journey east. I think Jay may have popped in a cassette by W.A.S.P., "The Last Command", with the song *Blind in Texas*.

West Texas was — and for the most part still is — very sparsely populated. Once you left El Paso, there were only a few rest-stops and gas stations along the interstate until you got to San Antonio.

It was just over 570 miles from El Paso to Killeen. Even at 110 mph, it's still five-and-a-half hours. No matter how fast you fly down long stretches of straight open road, it's still boring. Yes, the sign posts indicating miles to go to the next few towns or cities go by more quickly, but there isn't much else to do other than continue to follow the road. This is the perfect breeding ground for mischief. As the saying goes, "idle hands are the devil's tools."

The highway patrol agencies in many of the States seemed to all use the same type of car which had a distinctive headlight configuration and a red light attached to or next to the rearview mirror on the door or the A-pillar. I guess the single red light was more streamline than the cumbersome light-bar mounted on the roof. Nevertheless, this got me to thinking. We had a flashlight with a big — about 5-in. diameter — lens and Jay's car had rectangular headlights like the cop cars. I discovered I could take my red bandana and cover the lens of the flashlight thus making it look like a red light. I shared my thoughts with Jay and went on to say, "You know how when cops come up behind you, they come up all fast 'n' shit and get really close to your back bumper, almost like tailgating? Then they turn on the red-light and flashin' high-beams 'n' shit. I wonder if we could do that to some-one and get 'em to pull over?"

"Whaddya gonna to do once they're pulled over 'n' shit?"

"I hadn't thought about that. I suppose if someone actually does pull over, I say we see if he comes to a complete stop and if he does, we just take off. Even if he gets pissed and tries to chase us, I'm sure you can out run 'em 'n' shit."

Sounds like a really dumb idea, doesn't it? And we weren't even drunk. We hadn't had any alcohol since the dinner at Mario's brother's place, so we couldn't blame our stupidity on booze. Just goes to show you what the combination of testosterone, unbridled youth and boredom can lead to.

Anyway, we had time on our hands, we had a plan, now we just needed a hapless sucker. Driving at over a hundred miles an hour, it wasn't long before we noticed a pair of taillights in the distance ahead of us. Adrenaline was pumping. Hopefully this wasn't a cop or we'd get into some serious trouble.

Gaining on the car in front of us, I remarked, "Those don't look like cop taillights to me. Wanna try to fake 'em out and pull 'em over 'n' shit?"

"Yeah, man, let's go for it."

Like the AC/DC song, *Highway to Hell*, there's no stoppin' now.

I wrapped my bandana over the lens of the flashlight, turned it on to check that it was working, then shut it off. Jay came up to within a few feet of the car in front. After a few seconds, I rolled down the window, put the flashlight into position and said...

"Alright, man. Start flashin' your headlights", while I turned on the 'red' light.

We could see the driver look at his review mirror, then look over his shoulder, then start slowing down.

"Dude! He's slowin' down! Oh my god, I can't believe this is workin'! Fuckin' A, man!"

Jay kept doing a steady rhythmic high-low-high-low with his headlights while I kept the 'red' light steady as the driver continued to slow down then ultimately pulled over and stopped. At the moment when the other guy stopped, Jay hit the gas and we sped off into the darkness.

The other guy sat on the side of the road for a few seconds after we split. Jay was going pretty fast so I couldn't tell if that guy was trying to catch us or not.

Jay said, "Dude! I can't believe that totally fuckin' worked!"

"Hey, man. I'm thinkin' we should only do that to cars that are actually speeding 'n' shit, just to see what they'll do."

"Ok."

I know what you're thinking, 'Don't you guys know that everyone in Texas has guns?' Well, we were too impetuous to think about that.

Several miles down the road, we spotted another car. We decided to close in to where they were just beyond where the low-beams shined and pace them to see how fast they were going.

"Damn, only 60."

We could tell it wasn't a cop car so we just blasted right past that guy. The next guy, though, would be the guinea pig; he was doing about 75 when we paced him.

"You ready?"

"Yeah I am."

Jay rushed up to within a few feet of his rear bumper and kept it there for a few seconds. Before we could do the thing with the lights, the guy started to slow down.

"Hold up, man", I said to Jay. "Let's see what he's gonna do, first."

The guy slowed down to about 55 and kept it there for a while.

"Dude. I think he thinks we're cops 'n' shit. Why else would he slow down to 55?"

Jay said, "Let's do it", and with that, we lit the guy up. Sure enough, the guy starts slowing way down and pulls over. Like before, just as the guy had stopped, Jay whipped his Firebird off the shoulder back onto the road and hauled ass. This time, though, the other guy tried to chase us down.

"Whoa, dude. That guy's comin' after us 'n' shit", I said.

With confidence, Jay's calm tone had a hint of dismissive arrogance when he responded, "We'll see about that." Cue *Danger Zone* by Kenny Loggins.

Though it was dark, I didn't have to see him to "hear" the smirk he had on his face when he said that while accelerating northwards of 100 mph. He also cut the headlights so the other guy couldn't see our tail-lights but he turned on just the fog lights so we could see the road ahead. We obviously really pissed that guy off. Can you imagine? It's around 1:00 in the morning, you're probably about 30 miles from the nearest anything, you're speeding along a dark empty road when suddenly, a car with rectangular headlights imposingly comes up behind you, a red light comes on and lights start flashing. I mean, if it looks like a duck, sounds like a duck, and acts like a duck, why wouldn't you think it really was a duck? Then after you comply and pull over, what you thought was a cop car zooms past and you see that it was a red Firebird with a couple of douchebags in it laughing. How could you not be pissed? Relieved, maybe, that it wasn't a cop but pissed nonetheless.

* * *

Those shenanigans helped us to kill a couple of hours. But now, we were rapidly approaching the exit where we'd be making "a left turn at Albuquerque". Well, not Albuquerque, of course, but somewhere in East Pecos. Ha... East Pecos. What is this? The old West? Next thing you know, a Texas Ranger will be coming 'round the next bend with his posse to track us down for havin' rustled some cattle or something.

So, anyway, having gone about halfway across Texas, we were approaching the exit to take U.S. highway 190 east toward Killeen. A few miles before the exit, it started raining. Fortunately, it was only a light rain.

"Might wanna be cautious here" I mentioned to Jay. "My mom and I were stationed in Fort Sam Houston and Fort Bliss here in Texas. I've seen the rains here flood out roads 'n' shit in nothin' flat."

Jay nodded in acknowledgement never taking his gaze away from the road. Just so you know, those Army posts are in San Antonio and El Paso respectively.

The exit to the 190 really was in the middle of nowhere. The nearest anything was a lonely rest-area just under a half-mile east of the exit. Route 190 was a one-lane each way type road and much like every other road in west Texas, it was for the most part, an empty lonely road. We still had about 280 miles to go before we got into Killeen and Jay was eager to get there as quickly as possible so as to be with Leanne.

It was time for us to part ways with interstate 10, also known as the Christopher Columbus Transcontinental Highway. That road had conveyed us across the entire American southwest. We said our goodbyes to the 10 then turned onto route 190. The rain was like a real-life metaphor representing the washing away of what was before so as to have a clean start for what was to come.

With *Radar Love* by Golden Earring playing on the radio, Jay started out cautiously as route 190 welcomed us onto its pavement. It didn't take long, though, for Jay's lead foot to exercise its will on the accelerator. I was trying to catch a few z's, occasionally stirring and peering out the windshield in-between cat naps. Sometime during one of those moments of hazy wakefulness, I noticed we were going pretty fast considering it was raining. The road was making a long slow wide turn when I spotted a pair of headlights between some thin trees. I hadn't realized it yet but we had crossed over into east Texas.

Not to keep you in suspense but one of the peculiarities of Texas is that there is a distinct yet subtle natural, although I use that term loosely, boundary that distinguishes east Texas from west Texas. It's only noticeable during the day. You see, the west is all bleak and dry whereas the east is green and lush. Should you ever drive along route 190 during the day, you'll experience it. It's like you're driving along seeing desert and more desert, you blink, then everything is green. It's the weirdest thing.

Ok, so I saw these headlights and I noticed that they started moving onto route 190. Jay spotted them too and steered to avoid them. This was a recipe for a skid. The Firebird lost traction and started to slowly rotate left bringing the passenger side, my side, of the car to face the other car. I only had enough time to think, 'I wonder how much this is gonna hurt.'

Miraculously, the other car stopped just as Jay successfully corrected the skid. I was to live another day.

"Oh man!" I exclaimed. "Dude, I thought I was gonna cash out just now."

"Fuckin' *hours* of nothin'," responded Jay, "then suddenly in the middle of fuckin' *nowhere*, that **dick** almost crashed into us! What an *asshole*!"

Oh yeah, I should've mentioned that going hand in hand with his impatience, Jay had a volatile temper. I'd never seen him strike anyone but he wasn't one to back down in the face of a threat.

To help redirect his thoughts, I asked, "I wonder how far we are from Killeen? Did you see any sign posts 'n' shit?"

Jay answered, "I think it's still a ways. Maybe a hundred miles or so."

I didn't sleep that last hundred or so miles. Thinking about the near-crash experience prevented me from catching any more z's.

* * *

It was still dark and raining when we finally made it into Killeen. The only thing I remember when we got off the freeway was, just as Jay was getting ready to make a left turn, I commented that there was a Dunkin Donuts to my right. Jay immediately turned right into the donut shop parking lot.

Dunkin Donuts' popularity had been declining in California during that time and it had been a long time since there were any locations in central California. So, when Jay heard me mention that we were right next to one, he had to stop. It had been a while since we had eaten anything so, from what I recall, those were the best coffee and donuts ever. We asked the guy behind the counter where we could gas up and get a map of Killeen. He pointed us toward a local 7-eleven where we did just that; filled up and got a map. Jay had Leanne's address but didn't know how to get there because he'd never been there. She was living with her parents in family quarters on the Army post. I found it on the map and Jay was rearing to go.

"Dude, it's like three in the mornin'. We're gonna wake 'em up and they'll be all pissed 'n' shit."

"I'm not gonna knock on the door, I just wanna see where she lives and if her car's in the driveway."

I was anxious about this plan of his but I reservedly acquiesced. So, we went to the main gate at Fort Hood where gate security waved us in then saluted.

This would be a good time to mention that every personal automobile that belonged to a service member and their family was registered with the department of defense and issued a sticker which was affixed to the front bumper. When gate personnel saw and recognized that sticker, they just waved you in. Remember, this was the mid-80's, we didn't have anywhere near the problems with psychos like we have now. As for the gate guard saluting after waving us in, the stickers had different colors depending on the rank of the service member the car was registered to. Jay's father was a warrant officer.

So, with map in hand, we threaded our way to Leanne's housing area. The rain had let up quite a bit.

I said, "According to the map, it should only be a couple more streets then we turn left."

We slowly came upon the street Leanne lived on and Jay was getting more excited.

"Which one is it?", Jay asked.

"Let me get the flashlight... Ok, her house number's even so it should be on the left side. Stop for a second so I can see where we are 'n' shit."

I shined the flashlight on a house but, "I can't see the numbers from here."

"Gimme the flashlight", demanded Jay as he put the car in park. He stepped out of the car and walked up to one of the houses on the left to see what number it was. He came back and said, "We're a couple blocks away from her place."

We went two streets over then looked at the house numbers again. Jay stopped, smiled, and announced, "That's her car."

"Are you sure? Better double check the house number 'n' shit."

He parked the car and shut it off. We both stepped out of the car and carefully closed the doors so as not to disturb anyone. I stayed by the car while Jay, grinning ear to ear, went with the flashlight over to check the house number where Leanne's car was parked. He looked back at me and gave a big thumbs-up while nodding his head and still smiling. I couldn't recall the last time I'd seen him this happy. He then approached Leanne's car and looked through the windows, shining his flashlight onto the dash. We were close enough to a neighborhood street light to where I could see Jay's face. I watched his gleeful expression morph into heartbreaking disappointment. He remained frozen in that state for several seconds. He bowed his head slightly, shut off the flashlight, turned around, then came back to the Firebird. In silence, he opened the driver's door, stepped in, then gently closed it. I did the same on the passenger side. After a few moments I asked him what happened.

"When I looked at her dash, there was a picture of a dude... and it wasn't *me*."

* * *

So, yeah, it was kinda heavy.

Prior to his being with Leanne, Jay was a bit of a player. It's not my place to psychoanalyze him but I will relay my observations. After Jay had been involved with Leanne for a while, he seemed to mature and gave off a subtle yet noticeable sense of stability. She was the most positive influence on his development as a person. He had been telling me how much they loved each other and how close they were before her dad's duty station changed some months earlier to Fort Hood. He had gone on to say how they stayed in touch and expressed their love through letters and phone calls, how much they missed each other and how they yearned to see each other again. I could tell that he strived to be a better person because of her. He was so devoted to her that he didn't even flirt with any other chicks which was a huge departure from how he was before. By all accounts, Jay had every reason to believe that Leanne was "the one" and that she was "waiting" for him. She had not given him any reasons to doubt her sincerity and faithfulness. I was really taken aback by Jay's discovery.

"For real?", I asked. He nodded. "Sorry to hear that, man."

Making the kind of discovery he made the way that he did, the conflicting feelings and emotions Jay experienced must have seemed overwhelming. I could genuinely empathize with Jay for I had — with some subtle differences — actually been in that same situation myself; another story about another road-trip for another time. The disbelief, the anger, the denial, the betrayal, the doubt, the sense of loss, the uncertainty... At this moment, about the only thing we were certain of was that it was cold and wet outside, we were tired from the long drive, and we needed some rest.

I ultimately broke the silence asking, "How 'bout we get some sleep 'n' shit? I think I saw a motel just off post."

We decided to see about getting a room at the motel. Jay started the car, put it in gear, then slowly pulled away from Leanne's house. Boy, was I wiped. Though I felt bad for Jay, I couldn't wait to crash.

* * *

I woke up to someone knocking on the door. Jay answered. It was Leanne.

'What time is it?', I wondered as I sleepily scanned the room for the ubiquitous motel-room digital clock with the red LED numbers. I remember it being early, probably around 7:00 or 8:00 o'clock in the morning. I had done my share of late-night and all-night study sessions in college so I was no stranger to getting only a few hours of sleep. Nevertheless, since I figured Jay and Leanne had some issues they needed to settle and didn't need to air their dirty laundry in front of me, I would try and catch a few more z's. Jay went outside to speak with her and closed the door.

It must have been about an hour or so later when Jay woke me up and said, "Wake up, Mark, let's pack up our shit and get the fuck outta here."

I kinda played it off with him, letting him think I didn't know Leanne was there, "Hey, dude, who was it that came knockin' on the door this morning?"

"Leanne."

"How'd she know we were here?"

"After you crashed 'n' shit, I went back to her place and left a note on her car."

Told you I was wiped out. I didn't even notice Jay had left. He went on to say, "She saw it before she headed out to work then came straight here."

Jay gave me a full rundown of how she had remained faithful for as long as she could but her need for companionship and the seemingly endless state of their long-distance relationship — separated as they were — increased her feelings of hopelessness, thus allowing herself to let someone else into her heart all the while feeling guilty about it. They were both remarkably mature about the whole situation.

I couldn't help but to ask, "Did she say anything about bein' in touch with your parents 'n' shit?"

"Oh yeah. My parents called her AND her parents a bunch of times to find out if they'd heard anything about me 'n' shit; she never thought I'd just show up here without callin' her."

"Well, that's kinda obvious 'n' shit. But, go on."

"Yeah, I know, huh? Anyway, she called some of her and my friends in Fort Ord to find out what was goin' on and they told her about what went down in Salinas. They also told her that my parents were all super fuckin' pissed 'n' shit, especially my dad. They went over to their houses and threatened that they would go to the MP's if they didn't tell 'em where I was 'n' shit. She said they were really scared and that even their parents were pressurin' 'em to talk."

Just so you know, in the military, the family of a service member are classified as "dependents" and the service member is their "sponsor". As their sponsor, the service member is responsible for any and all actions, including any improprieties, committed by the dependents while on post. The military commanders do not have authority over civilian dependents but they do have authority over their sponsor. To maintain order, should a dependent violate a regulation, the sponsor is punished, not the dependent. The severity of the punishment could lead to reduction in rank or even a dishonorable discharge.

"I figured as much", I said.

"Dude, you were so totally right about not tellin' anyone about what we were doin' 'n' shit. And my parents even goin' over to my friends' houses to harass 'em 'n' shit. But, like you said, they couldn't talk about somethin' that they don't know about."

"Good thing Eric's dad had retired from the Army and they left for Kansas before this all went down." I quickly asked, "Ok, so, what about now that Leanne knows where you are 'n' shit? Will she and her parents keep quiet?"

"Leanne saw the note before her parents did so they still don't know anything. Besides, they know what my parents are like and probably wouldn't tell 'em anything anyway. And I totally trust Leanne to keep quiet 'n' shit."

With a sigh of relief, I said, "Well that's good."

* * *

It was a cold crisp sunny morning in Killeen. Last night's rain was long gone and the light of day flooded the town, now buzzing with activity. Jay liked to keep his Firebird clean so after we packed up the car, checked out of the motel, and grabbed a bite to eat, we went in search of a car wash. The chick behind the counter at the diner where we had breakfast recommended a do-it-yourself place just down the street. Ya know, it's pretty hard to wash your car at one of those places that has the high-pressure style water nozzle and not get yourself wet. I wasn't too thrilled about starting my day with damp jeans and numb fingers. I decided to view this as another metaphoric moment. Jay washing his car was cathartic. He was, again, washing away the past so as to begin the rest of his life fresh and clean.

We fueled up the sparkling red Firebird then hopped onto interstate 14, which just so happens to begin in Killeen, heading east. I'd like to think Van Halen's *Panama* was playing on the radio as we put Fort Hood, Leanne, and the rest of Jay's past behind us.

It was December 23, next stop was Clay Center, Kansas, where Eric and his dad moved to, some 630 miles up interstate 35.

Merry Christmas Eric

After some 10-miles down I-14, we headed north-bound on I-35. The entire length of I-14 stretches from Killeen to Belton, just over 10 miles; go figure.

Because east Texas was more densely populated than west Texas, driving 100+ mph was much more risky. There weren't many opportunities to speed between Temple and Waco, and though Waco to Fort Worth had a few more open stretches, they were only a few more. This, combined with his lack of sleep from the previous night, made Jay weary so he asked me to take over driving as we got ready to leave the northern outskirts of Fort Worth on our way to Oklahoma City.

"No problem, man. And, sorry, again, about the shit that went down with Leanne. At least it wasn't as fucked up as what Tanya in Oregon did to me."

Ok, I had touched on this story in the previous chapter and I know you're curious so, here's the Reader's Digest version:

While I was still living on Fort Ord back in the spring of 1985, I met a chick named Tanya who was visiting from Oregon and the spitting image of Eva LaRue. After she went back home, we stayed in touch. I was thinking about making a road trip with a friend of mine, Ernesto, to go see her so I asked her if she was still single and receptive to a visit from me, and if she could hook my friend up with a chick. She said she was and she could. So just days before Ernesto and I were set to embark upon this trip, I called her again to make sure everything was still cool which she confirmed it was, and she couldn't wait to see me. So, after driving nearly 500 miles from Monterey California, Ernesto and I pulled into Klamath Falls, Oregon, at this pre-agreed diner and Tanya eventually showed up with some friends and her boyfriend. We had trekked all this way and her response was, "I never thought you'd really come here." That was one of the most awkward trips I'd ever taken. Like I said before, another story for another time.

So anyway, after topping off the tank, I settled in behind the wheel of Jay's Firebird for a leisurely drive up I-35 to Oklahoma City. *Slow Ride* by Foghat must've been on the radio.

We topped the tank off rather frequently. You see, being Californians, we've gotten into the habit of not letting our tank go below the halfway point because in the event of a severe earthquake, gas stations may be out of operation for some days.

Most of the topography was pretty flat north of Fort Worth, after all, most of the center of the United States was cattle country; lots of grazing land. Fortunately for me, the sun went down shortly after we left Fort Worth. Unfortunately, the radio station I was listening to faded into the distance.

Jay had brought all his cassettes which we played throughout the journey. Fortunately, we shared the same taste in music. His stuff included some 80's glam bands such as Mötley Crüe, Poison, and Dokken to hard rock like Sabbath, Ozzy, and WASP, to metal like Metallica and Slayer, and everything in between. I didn't mind listening to cassettes at all but I sometimes preferred the radio for the following reasons: for one thing, more variety. Unlike a store-bought cassette which has a single album from one artist, the DJ mixes songs from several different artists. The other thing; local radio stations would broadcast newsworthy information such as flash flooding, road closures, tornadoes, etc. Way out in the sticks as we were most of the time, we frequently drove for an hour with nothing but dead air between decent stations and had to rely on cassettes. In case you didn't know, rock music was pretty much exclusively on FM which was a mixed blessing. You see, FM broadcasts a stereo signal and the sound quality is superior to AM. Also, FM is not sensitive to underpasses unlike AM which cuts out. The disadvantage is that the FM signal doesn't travel far. AM travels much farther but lacks the fidelity of FM.

Each time I ejected a cassette to change it, I would slowly turn the dial from one end to the other in search of a radio station. If I found one, I kept it tuned in until it eventually faded away. If I didn't find a suitable station, I'd put in another cassette. Rinse, repeat... I managed to tune in an "ok" station as we got closer to Oklahoma City. It was around 9:00 o'clock at night and Jay was stirring as we were on our approach to the city. I asked him, "You wanna top off before we enter the city or after we pass through it?"

"The other side", a la The Doors, *Break On Through (To the Other Side)*.

I couldn't blame him for being terse. It was cold outside, Christmas was on the horizon and his heart was broken. He was at the point of just wanting to get this trip over with.

* * *

I-35 took us east of the city's center. At that time of night and being a couple days before Christmas, there was no traffic. Just beyond the city limits to the north of Oklahoma City was a truck-stop where we stopped to top off the Firebird's tank. We preferred fueling at truck stops mainly because they were more likely than random stations along the highway or within towns to take the Discover card Jay lifted from his mom's wallet. I don't think we encountered a single restaurant on this journey that took Discover. Back then, though a few places utilized the electronic card readers, pretty much all the stations still had the credit card imprinter machines that used carbon paper slips. The merchant had to mail the slips to the bank which meant there was an inherent processing delay. Every time we used the Discover card, we hoped the merchant had the older style machine. If they had the magnetic strip reader, we crossed our fingers. We were rather fortunate in that, of those merchants who accepted Discover and used the electronic reader, none of them were notified of anything irregular, which in turn reassured us that Jay's parents hadn't noticed the card went missing.

While we were gassing up the Firebird, a pickup truck pulled up to the other side of the gas pump island. Two foxes stepped out and got ready to gas up their truck. This will sound cliché but they looked like a couple of country girls who had a bit of a naughty streak. If the radio in the Firebird were on then *Turbo Lover* by Judas Priest would've been playing.

One of them stayed by the truck, looked over, smiled, and said "Nice car", as her friend went inside the minimart to pre-pay for the gas.

I smiled back and answered, "Thanks."

"How fast does it go?"

I couldn't help being a suggestive smartass when I responded, "Oh, it'll quickly get up there pretty far, **and** keep goin' for a long time."

She smiled and just then, her friend came back and, looking at our car's license plate, said, "I see y'all are from California."

I nodded.

"Where in California?"

"We left Los Angeles day before yesterday."

"Ooo, L.A. Y'all visitin' or just passin' through?"

Smiling again, I replied, "Just passin' through but if there's a reason for us to stick around for a little bit", turning my head toward Jay, "we may be open to changin' our itinerary 'n' shit."

The first girl picked up the gas pump nozzle, placed the tip just inside the truck's filler neck, asked, "Would a party be a good enough reason for y'all to stay a while", then pushed the nozzle all the way into the truck. It reminded me of that Whitesnake song, *Slide It In*.

Jay finally spoke up, "What kinda party?"

"We's on our way to a big ol' shindig at the Hudson place..."

As she went on I was starting to feel like Rod Serling was about to step out from behind one of the gas pumps and tell us we were entering the Twilight Zone. Something just wasn't adding up. I got a vibe similar to the one I had when I pulled into that gas station in Salinas, the difference being visions of "Deliverance". Why would a couple of hot local chicks on their way to a party extend an invitation to a couple of random dudes from out of State whom they met in the middle of the night at a truck stop? We didn't even know each other's names. I mean, don't get me wrong, I dig chicks who are forward but in this case, there was something intangible that unsettled me. Besides, what sort of folks throw a big ol' party on a Tuesday night?

When they finished talking, I said to them, "Before I address your invitation, please forgive my rudeness and allow me to introduce ourselves; I'm Mark and this is Jay."

The first chick replied, "I'm Jenny and this is Sheila."

"Charmed. Ladies, may I consult with my colleague for a moment?"

After Jay and I walked around to the other side of his Firebird, before I could say a word, he excitedly whispered, "Dude, we're *totally* gonna get laid 'n' shit; score us some nasty country girl ass."

"Whoa, man, rein it in."

I really felt for Jay, especially now that he was on the rebound from Leanne, but these chicks...

"I can't put my finger on it, man", I said to him, "but there's somethin' not right about this."

"Come on, man, relax. It'll be fun. Let's just go to their party. It's probably on a farm where there's a barn 'n' shit and we just bend 'em over some hay bales and bang 'em like farm animals."

After a moment, it came to me, "I have a better idea. Just follow my lead 'n' shit ... and remember rule number 1."

We came back around the car and, smiling, I said to the ladies, "Ya know, it'll be really hard to get to know each other at a big ol' shindig, and we've taken a real likin' to y'all two. We'd kinda like to get to know y'all better before we go to the party with you. On our way here, we noticed a Howard Johnson's on the interstate; y'all know which one I'm talkin' 'bout?"

They nodded and their expressions were kinda blank. I quickly suggested, "What say we get a room there? Nothin' heavy, just talk, maybe mess around a little if you want."

Sheila then asked, "Y'all fixin' to stay the night?"

Still flirting, I answered, "Well, as long as we have a reason to stay, might as well make it last for the whole night. It wouldn't be gentlemanly for us to impose on y'all for accommodations so we respectfully ask you graciously accept our hospitality and follow us down the interstate to the hotel."

"Well me and Sheila don't wanna be late for the shindig…"

That was the clincher. If they really wanted us to satisfy their carnal desires, why would they prefer to lure us to some alleged party rather than come with us to the hotel? To help them save face, I offered a proposal, "Tell ya what…"

I got some paper and a pen out of the car, handed them to Jenny and said, "Here. Write down the directions to the shindig and the phone number of the place. Y'all then go on ahead and we'll meet you there right after Jay and I get a room at the Howard Johnson's. Shouldn't take more than an hour."

They looked at each other and Jenny said, "Alright."

The chicks wrote down the directions and a phone number then handed back the paper and pen. We all said we'd see each other soon while exchanging eye winks and blown kisses. Just as they drove off I shared my suspicions and opinions with Jay.

"No way, man. Ya think? I mean... I don't know. I suppose you could be right 'n' shit."

I then had him follow me into the minimart where I approached the guy, an older gentleman, behind the register and asked him, "'Scuse me, you got a local map?"

"Yup. Here ya go", he said putting it on the counter.

On top of the map, I laid the paper with the directions the chick wrote and said, "I'm tryin' to find *this* place", pointing to the paper. "Can you help me find it on the map?"

The guy reads the directions then said, "Nope. 'T'ain't on this map."

"Well, do the directions make sense?"

"Yup", he said. "They're to the ol' Hudson place but it ain't on the map 'cause it's on a private dirt road."

"What can you tell me about the Hudson place?"

"It's been abandoned for years and kids sometimes go out there for target shootin' and to party on the weekends."

"Is there a phone out there," I asked.

"Not one that works. There ain't even electricity out there."

I looked over at Jay and asked, "Wanna try and dial the number?"

He looked at me for a moment, turned toward the door and started walking. I started out right behind him and on our way out, said to the guy behind the register, "Thanks and have a nice evening."

We went back to the Firebird, Jay behind the wheel and me in the passenger seat. He was understandably disappointed and pissed. I was concerned he would do something rash or reckless.

I said to him, "If you're still curious, we could go as far as the dirt road for a looksee 'n' shit."

I could tell he thought about it for a moment but ultimately decided against it. Maybe Leanne's influence went deeper than I had originally thought. The pre-Leanne Jay would've surrendered to his primal impulse and exacted revenge.

"God damn fuckin' bullshit!", he exclaimed. "Let's just get the fuck outta here!"

And, so, we got back on I-35 north and put Oklahoma City behind us, its lights gradually fading into the darkness as the miles rolled by. *Here I Go Again* by Whitesnake may have been on the radio. We would be in Clay Center in about 300 miles.

* * *

With how disappointing things had been during the previous 24 hours, we hadn't been thinking about how things were unfolding for Eric, but we would be hearing all about it soon enough. According to the map, we would have to transition onto I-135, just before we got into Wichita. With it being nighttime and the road being straight and flat, Jay's lead foot was slowly getting heavier and we found ourselves cruising at 100+ mph on our way to Wichita. It was my turn to try and catch some z's. I had to keep myself from leaning up against the window because it was so cold outside. Fortunately, since the road was pretty straight and flat, the car didn't move much from side to side. Cradled in the bucket seat, drifting between sleep and wakefulness, dream state and reality, the hum of the engine creating a sort of white noise while the ever so subtle irregularities in the road gently rocked me into slumber.

As we approached Wichita, we saw a sign for the turnoff to McConnell air force base. We saw quite a number of military bases along the way but didn't think much about them. Living on a military base is very different from what civilians are accustomed to. For one thing, seeing tanks driving down the street was normal. If you park your car someplace where you're not supposed to, it may get squished by a tank — that's no joke — and it would be the fault of the person that parked the car. Everything is clean and orderly. There are no homeless people loitering about, there's no graffiti, no litter, and everyone's quarters are well maintained. When my mother first joined the Army, it was a bit of an adjustment. I didn't realize how assimilated I had become, let alone how much I would miss living on post, until I moved to Los Angeles fulltime.

It was probably around 11:00 o'clock at night when we drove through the heart of Wichita on I-135.

Jay said, "We've got enough gas to get us to Salina 'n' shit."

"Ok", I replied. It was only 90 miles away. Maybe enough time for a few more winks. By the time we get there, it'll probably be Christmas Eve, early morning that is.

In the minimart at the gas station where we fueled up in Salina, we got a map of Kansas and I asked the guy behind the counter, "Would you have a detailed map of Clay Center?"

"Nah, sorry." Then, sounding more puzzled than quizzical, he asked, "Why would you wanna go there?"

The way he asked that question made me want to raise an eyebrow.

I tried not to hesitate when I answered, "To visit an old friend of ours for Christmas."

"Where're you boys from?"

"California."

"He must be a really good friend."

'Curious', I thought to myself, nevertheless, I answered, "Yeah he is".

The guy wasn't far from the mark, though. Had we not chosen to visit Eric, we could've caught I-44 in Oklahoma City which would've taken us straight to St. Louis where we would've caught I-70 to Indianapolis; a route that would've saved about 175 miles and quite a bit of time.

Jay and I exited the minimart, approached the Firebird, opened the doors, took off our coats, tossed them in the backseat, then got inside the warm cabin. Jay fired up the engine then we got back onto I-135, aka, U.S. Hwy. 81, north for another 30 miles before we turned east on U.S. 24. It was then about another 20 miles until we came upon Clay Center's main drag, Kansas State route 15, also known as 6th Street.

* * *

It was probably around 12:30 at night when we came to the intersection of U.S. 24 and State route 15 which had a traffic light. We turned right, down onto the main drag which went into the center of that sleepy small town. I didn't know it at the time but Clay Center was and still is a genuine small town.

Jay and I had no clue where Eric's family was within the town so we just kept rolling down 6th Street figuring we'd see something like a gas station. We slowly approached an intersection with a traffic signal and stopped. Looking around, there was nobody on the street. Everything was closed.

"This town looks completely dead 'n' shit", Jay remarked. "How're we gonna find Eric?"

"Someone's *gotta* be awake in this town... I have an idea; let's try 'n' find a police station. I've never been to a place yet where the police station closes. After all, criminals don't work regular hours 'n' shit."

Fortunately, the police station was in the center of town along the main drag. When the light turned green, we continued south on the main drag to the next traffic light.

Pointing to the right at a building on the corner that had a police cruiser parked in front of it, I said, "Hey, man, I'll betcha that's it."

We turned the corner then parked next to the cop car. We instantly learned how cold it was outside when we opened the Firebird's doors. We grabbed our jackets from the back seat, put them on, then walked up the walkway into the station. Inside, there was a middle-aged chick manning the front desk and one deputy. They both appeared at once surprised and suspicious at our arrival.

The chick asked, "Can I help you?"

She spoke with deliberation, as though she quickly formulated what she was going to say before actually saying it then letting it come out at a steady pace. I answered, "I certainly hope so. We're tryin' to track down a friend of ours who moved here last week, figurin' we'd surprise him with a visit for Christmas, but we don't have his address."

Listening to myself now saying what I said back then, it's no wonder that the deputy and the desk chick were suspicious of us. Eric and his father moved before the incident in Salinas. Their plan was to stay with Eric's grandmother on his father's side until they found their own place. Once they moved into their permanent residence, Eric would write to me, Jay, and everyone else, what his new address was. So, we never got Eric's grandmother's address because it never seemed necessary or relevant.

Anyway, I went on to say to the front desk chick, "However, we do know that our friend is stayin' with his grandmother and his family's last name. Would you happen to have a local phone book we could look at?"

The chick stood up and went over to a cabinet where they kept the phone book. While she did that, she asked, "Where're you boys from?"

"California."

"Comin' all the way here from California... must be a really good friend."

'Gee, that's kinda what the minimart guy said', I thought to myself just then.

"Yeah he is," I answered.

The complete absence of any open businesses kinda clued me in that Clay Center was a small town but gazing upon the phone book really helped put into perspective just how small it was. The desk chick picked up what looked like a pamphlet about the size of an instruction manual for a claw-hammer in seven languages. This thing could not have been more than maybe a dozen pages. 'That's their phone book?' I thought to myself. Jay and I look at each other with wide eyes for just a moment.

The desk chick then walked up to the counter, laid the phone book down, opened it, leaned over and asked, "What's the last name?"

I told her, then she turned to the page where it would be found if it was listed.

"Here it is", she said, turning the book around so it was right-side-up for us and pointing at the name. An address was printed next to the name. I wrote it down.

"Would you have a detailed map I can look at that includes this address?"

"We got a map on the wall back here", she said pointing to an area behind her, "but it's easy to get to."

"Ok, how do we get there?"

What followed was... well, you need to hear it to believe it, and she always spoke in that steady deliberate pace.

"Well, start by headin' east 'til you get to the highway…"

"What highway?"

"This one right here", she said pointing at 6th Street which, in all fairness, is Hwy. 15.

"You mean the street we took to get here?"

"Yes. So, start by headin' east 'til you get to the highway, then head north."

"Ok, so left onto the main drag."

"This ain't the main highway, that's too far north, I'm talkin' about this highway right here", pointing again at 6th Street. "So, start by headin' east 'til you get to the highway, then head north."

That's when it hit me; her mind worked like those old computers with the punch cards. You had to load all the punch cards into the computer before you could run the program. If you interrupted the program, you couldn't just resume it, you had to reload all the punch cards then restart the program from the beginning. I was dreading this.

She went steadily on, "You'll be goin' north for a while past the main highway 'til you get to Lane Street. When you get to Lane Street you'll need to head east and the house will be about halfway down on the north side of the street."

That is, I think it was Lane St. I cannot recall which street it was, only that it was one of the little neighborhood streets north of U.S. 24. I finished writing down the directions and said, "Ok, got it."

I looked over at Jay and said, "Ready to head out?"

"Yup."

"Ok." I turned to the desk chick and said, "Thanks for your help."

"You're welcome."

After Jay and I got back in his Firebird, I said, "Dude. Did you check out that tiny phone book?"

"I know, huh."

"And what about how that chick talked all robotic 'n' shit?"

"Yeah she did. Pretty weird."

So, while following the directions, we rehashed what just went down in the police station. It seemed to take less time to find the house than it took for the chick to give us the directions.

It was around 1:00 o'clock in the morning and the house looked totally dark. Just as we stepped out of the Firebird, we noticed there was a car driving north on the main drag passed the street we were on.

Jay said, "Dude. I think that was the cop car."

"I wouldn't doubt it. I'll bet you us comin' into town is probably the most action they've seen all day 'n' shit."

We went up the walkway to get a closer look at the house numbers and listen for any sounds emanating from the house. It was silent. In fact, that entire street was pretty dark and completely silent. We then saw the cop car again, this time it was heading south on the main drag. Back on the sidewalk, we contemplated what to do next.

I suggested, "We should find a place to stay the night 'n' shit then come back in the morning."

"Where should we go?"

"I say we go back to the cop station and ask the desk chick where the nearest motel is."

"Ok."

And just as we got into the Firebird, we saw the cop car again, going north on the main drag, again. I guess we really were the only game in town.

I quipped, "There he goes again. He's probably totally bored. Maybe we shoulda asked him to be our escort 'n' shit."

We turned around, went back to 6th Street, aka Hwy. 15, and headed south, back into downtown to the station. The cop car wasn't there which meant it was still out on patrol, probably looking for us. We went inside…

"Y'all back already? Couldn't find it?" asked the desk chick.

"We found it but it looked like everyone was asleep and we didn't want to wake them so we figured we'd get a room at a motel. Is there one around here?"

"Well, there're two; a nice one and a not-so-nice one."

"Which one's closer?"

"Well, that'd be the nice one."

"Ok. How do we get there?"

"Well, start by headin' east 'til you get to the highway…"

'Oh god, not this again!' I thought to myself. The look on Jay's face told me we were thinking the same thing. It was borderline agonizing listening to her dictate instructions and I knew if I interrupted her, she'd start over and we would begin our descent into madness. I started imagining we'd be there so long that the sun would start coming up.

After she finally finished with, "…and it's called the Cedar Court", we thanked her, went back to the car, and set out for the motel. Once again, it seemed like the drive to the motel took less time than writing down the directions; the drive took us less than three minutes. When we got there, it looked like it was closed. Upon closer inspection they had a sign on the door that read, "Please knock loud", which we did… for what seemed like ten minutes. We kept knocking in the hopes that someone would come to the door and answer because we really dreaded going back to the police station and asking the desk chick for directions to the "not so nice" place.

Finally, we saw a light come on inside the office and a guy came to the door.

Opening it only slightly, he asked, "What can I help you with?"

"We'd like a room with two beds if you got one."

He opened the door further saying, "Oh. Ok. At this hour. Yeah, I got a room. Need two beds. Come on in. Let me turn on s'more lights…"

We obviously woke this poor guy up from a deep sleep. He looked like he may have been in his 60s. He continued to speak but he wasn't mumbling or muttering. He spoke to us as well as to himself in the same tone.

"…Gonna need to fill out this registration card. I forgot to turn the heat down. How you gonna pay?"

Jay reached into his pocket, pulled out his wallet, took out the Discover card, then handed it to the guy, "Here you go."

The dude looked at it and asked, "What's this?"

"It's a Discover card, you know, a credit card."

"Ain't never seen one o' these before. Is this like a Master Charge?"

This dude was really old school. "Master Charge" was the original name of "MasterCard" before it changed in 1979. This was definitely one of those times where we had to use cash.

We got a room, parked the Firebird in front of it, then went inside to crash out for the night. It would've been kismet if the song *Carry on Wayward Son* by Kansas were playing on the radio.

* * *

I awoke to a room that was slightly illuminated by curtains glowing from the morning sun. I rolled over and looked at the clock. I don't remember what time it was but I recall it seemed early. I would wager it was between 8:00 and 9:00 in the morning.

"Jay. You up?"

"Yeah I am."

"When do you wanna get ready to head over to Eric's 'n' shit?"

"Anytime you're ready, man."

I was eager to go see Eric but, because it was Christmas Eve day, I figured he and his family would be sleeping in. I was in that state where, when you wake up in the morning, you're comfy and want to indulge in resting more but your mind is alert and restless. I stirred around in bed some more, stretched, and imagined what our reunion with Eric would be like.

I finally said to Jay, "I'm gonna take a shower, change clothes, 'n' shit".

Just as I got up, he said, "Sounds like a plan", and also got up.

We were so wiped out the previous night that we left our bags in the Firebird's trunk. We got dressed and opened the door. The sun was shining brightly in a clear deep blue sky. The air was still and really brisk making our breath quite visible. Jay opened the trunk, my bag was on top of Jay's so I took it out first then when Jay tried to take out his bag, it didn't move.

"The hell?" he remarked, "It's stuck."

Giving in to his impatient nature, he firmly grasped the strap and sharply yanked on it. The bag came out of the trunk along with a shower of clear shards.

I examined the shards and said, "Dude, that's ice."

The Firebird's trunk apparently leaked and water, probably from the rain and the car wash, had collected in the bottom of the trunk. Last night's temperature obviously dropped below freezing.

We went back inside the warm motel room and got ourselves ready to head over to Eric's.

* * *

The Firebird was all packed up and we had checked out of the motel. Before we departed, Jay picked out a Megadeth tape to play on the stereo — I think it was *Peace Sells... but Who's Buying?*.

In a tone that reflected his annoyance, Jay said, "This place is *way* too fuckin' quiet and needs to be shaken up. When we get outta the parkin' lot, I'm gonna crank this shit up full blast", a la the movie "Footloose".

It was around 10:00 o'clock, we put on our shades, rolled down the windows, cranked up the heat, and put the cassette in the stereo. We were only about two minutes from Eric's place and with Megadeth blasting, we slowly cruised up 9th Street then made a left onto Lane. We noticed a few folks peering out their windows as we casually rolled by exuding attitude, like we were the best thing to ever hit this two-bit Podunk town. Man, we were such assholes. We parked in front of, what we hoped — we still didn't really know — was, Eric's place, shut off the Firebird, stepped out, went up the walkway and knocked on the door. An older chick we didn't recognize answered and said, "Yes?"

"Is Eric here?"

"Why yes, he is, and you are?"

"We're friends of his from back home."

"Oh goodness, please come on in out of the cold. Have you boys had breakfast?"

"Not yet", I answered. This had to be Eric's grandmother.

She called out to him saying, "Eric! You got some visitors!"

The look on his face as he entered the room was priceless. "OH MY GOD! No frickin' way! I can't believe you guys are here!"

Eric usually used much more profanity and would've exclaimed, 'No fuckin' way' but he had to check his language in grandma's house.

I couldn't help but be a smartass and say, "Well, we happened to be passin' by and I figured we'd stop off and wish you a Merry Christmas."

"DUDE! You're really frickin' here! And is the Night Machine out front?!"

"Nah, we drove Jay's Firebird."

"Now Eric", his grandmother interrupted, "how 'bout you introduce me to your friends?"

"Sorry Gran, this is Mark and Jay from California."

"All the way from California? Y'all must be really good friends."

Was this another coincidence or was a thematic pattern emerging?

"Hi, boys. Y'all can call me Billy."

"Pleased to meet you."

Getting right to the point, she asked, "Now what say we rustle y'all up some breakfast?"

"Yes, if you please, we ain't eaten since yesterday."

We readied ourselves to gorge on the first home cooked meal we'd had since California; eggs, bacon, sausage, hot cakes, hash browns, steak — it was cattle country after all. We joined Eric and his dad around the dining table and got caught up on what all had gone down. Eric started off...

"I heard from Smurf that your dad beat you up in Salinas and you've been hidin' out but I never thought in a million years you'd come out here."

I replied, "It wasn't quite like that." I paused for a moment and turned toward Jay, "You wanna tell him?"

"You go ahead and tell him."

I gave him a look that said, 'everything?' to which he nodded 'yeah'.

So, I told him the story. As I was relaying it, he would ask for more details in some areas like the chase in Salinas and the chicks in Oklahoma City, and occasionally remarked, "Man, wish I was there."

I finished with, "...and so, we kept blastin' Megadeth right up until we parked in front of your house."

"Man, that's so cool. If I was still living in California I totally woulda gone with you guys."

I responded, "Probably not. We woulda kept you in the dark just like everyone else."

Eric's father, Rick, understood why Jay and I exercised a communication blackout and Eric even said, "Yeah, man", looking at Jay, "your parents are all way totally pissed, wacked out crazy. Smurf told me all about it. They came over to his house and threatened him and his parents with the MPs if he didn't tell 'em where you were."

He reflected for a moment then said, "Yeah, he woulda talked if he knew."

Rick spoke up, "That's just plain bullshit", then looking at Jay, "what your parents did and the way they're actin'." Then, looking at me, he continued, "And Mark, good thing you were there to make sure Jay and his car stayed safe."

Both of Eric's parents seemed to really like me and must have figured that I was a good role model and a good influence on him. I mean, I had graduated high school, and was enrolled at UCLA which was more than what lots of other characters Eric considered befriending had achieved. His parents trusted me with him even when it came to road trips; a couple of years earlier, I took Eric down to L.A. with me for a couple of days.

Anyway, the grandmother spoke up, "Well, boys, that's quite an adventure, somethin' to tell your kids and grandkids. Would y'all like to stay for Christmas?"

"Sure would. Thanks for the invitation."

"Of course. Well, if you're done with breakfast, how 'bout you bring in your bags and I'll show you where y'all be stayin'."

We went back out to Jay's Firebird to get our bags, brought them in, then were led upstairs to a partially finished attic where we set them down.

Eric said, "Hey guys, how 'bout we head into town, I need to get some cigarettes."

He wasn't old enough to buy them but Jay was.

We got into the Firebird with Eric in the backseat and made our way to 6th Street; the main drag. For

Jay and I, this was the first time we could clearly see the small town of Clay Center... and, man, was it a small town. It was even the subject of an article by Richard Hornik titled "Small-Town Blues" published in the Monday, March 27, 1989 edition of TIME Magazine. I was certain the dorms at UCLA house more people than this entire town's population. The first traffic light we came to was at the intersection with U.S. 24. A few short blocks later was the next light at Court Street. The sight I saw galvanized my assessment that this was as stereotypical a small town as you could get. We were stopped at the north-east corner of the town square. The town square was one city block with a traffic light at each of the four corners. The entire square was lawn with two buildings on it. The main building slightly set back from center in the city block was three stories, made of stone, and had a large clock tower on top. When I saw this, it totally reminded me of the movie, "Back to the Future". The other building was the police station I mentioned from the previous night with the one cop car out front. At the next light, on the south-east corner from the town square, cattycorner from the police station was the new car dealer with only one new car in the showroom. A little further down was a gas station with a minimart where we pulled in to top off the tank and get some cigarettes.

"I'll bet you no one in this whole town's ever heard of Discover 'n' shit", Jay grumbled.

I went inside with him and, sure enough, when Jay handed the Discover card to the clerk, he asked, "What's this?"

Oh boy. Jay and I gave each other that, 'I told you so' look.

Jay knew the routine down pat by now, "It's a credit card just like MasterCard. If you don't accept it, no problem, I got cash."

The clerk pondered for a moment, "Discover... Y'all ain't from around here, are you?"

Can you see where this is going?

"No. We drove here from Los Angeles, California."

Get ready...

"L.A.? What are y'all doin' way out here?"

Wait for it...

"We're visitin' a friend of ours who lives here."

...and...

"Must be a really good friend."

WTF! Jay and I looked at each other with that, 'you've *got* to be fucking *kidding* me' kind of look. I had to investigate this so I said to the guy, "Dude, you're like the fourth person in 24-hours who's been all, 'where're you from', and we're all, 'L.A.', and they're all, 'why're you way out here', and we're all, 'visitin' a friend', and they're all, 'must be a really good friend'. What's the deal?"

"Y'all are from L.A.. Folks from L.A. *never* come here. This is the middle of Kansas, there ain't nothin' to do here and we ain't got nothin' worth seein'. I ain't never met anyone that lives in L.A. until just now with y'all. This is the most interestin' thing that's happened to me all week."

Woah, talk about conflicted feelings. I felt flattered and depressed at the same time.

"That explains it", I replied. "Well, Merry Christmas and have a nice day."

"Merry Christmas to you too, sir."

As Jay and I stepped out of the minimart, I saw a payphone. On closer examination, I noticed a sticker affixed just above the pushbutton keypad that read, "Please dial all seven digits." I initially thought this was really odd until I reminded myself that back in the day, telephones were wired to exchanges and the numbers started with the first two letters of the exchange followed by five digits. For those of you who watch old movies and TV shows, you may hear someone say their number is Klondike 5, 2323. In this example, the exchange is Klondike and if you lived within the service range of that exchange, you'd only need to dial 5-2323, otherwise you'd have to dial "all seven digits" where the first two letters of Klondike (KL) correspond to the numbers 55 on a telephone, hence the full number was 555-2323. Anyway, looking at the notice sticker on this payphone led me to believe that within the last year or so, the number of active telephone numbers within the service area exceeded some sort of maximum and now everyone had to dial the entire number. If we were in North Carolina, I'd say this place had to be Mayberry.

Back in the car, I turned to the backseat and asked Eric, "So, man, anything to do or see 'round here?"

"*Fuck* no, man. This place it *totally* fuckin' Deadsville. I can't even *begin* to tell you how fuckin' *bored* I am here. And *everyplace* else is at *least* 50 fuckin' miles away. I didn't wanna come out here in the *first* place and now that we've been here only a couple of days, I'm *really* dyin' to leave. I kinda wish I were goin' with you guys 'n' shit. I actually wish we were all back in California."

* * *

Eric was having a rough time adjusting to the change. Moving is never easy. Military families move all the time. Though they know the process, how to do it, and what to expect, it's still not easy. And for families with school aged children, it's extra difficult, especially if the move happens during the school year.

We drove around the town a bit and, sure enough… nothing. The fact that it was Christmas Eve may have contributed to the apparent lack of activity on the streets, sidewalks, and amongst the businesses. Who knows, maybe after Christmas, the town will come back to life. Jay and I, though, were not going to stick around long enough to find out. We decided to blaze out of there that Saturday, December 26. Meanwhile, we made the best out of staying with Eric and his family at is grandmother's place.

While the three of us were hanging out, I noticed how Jay was including me in his confidential talks with Eric. That's when I knew he had endowed the same level of trust in me that he had with Eric.

Eric's grandmother was a genuine traditionalist. The images your mind conjures when you hear the words, "old fashioned Christmas" will set the scene better than any description I can write covering the next fifty pages. In fact, what stood out about it was it was so idyllic that nothing about it was remarkable. Let me put it another way. By nature, we humans tend to retain unpleasant memories (e.g., the last time you got a traffic ticket) rather than delightful ones (e.g., the last time you got a parking spot at the mall that was next to the entrance). And, you know how at most every family Christmas there's at least one thing that's unpleasant, be it obvious like that uncle who always gets drunk and acts like a dick to everyone, or subtle like the gravy that's just a tad bit too lumpy for you. Well, there was none of that for me at Christmas in 1987.

The first night sleeping at their house was a different story. Upstairs, in the partially finished attic, a couple of cots with blankets were prepared for Jay and me, and there was an oil-filled portable radiant electric heater. I say partially finished because there was a rudimentary floor but no insulation in the rafters. Pointing to the heater, I asked, "Do I need to set the temperature on this or anything?"

"Nah, it's all automatic."

"Ok."

It was really cold that night and the heater didn't seem to be helping. We were rather uncomfortable. The next morning at breakfast, Billy greeted us with, "Merry Christmas" followed by, "How'd you boys sleep?"

"Well, Billy, it was a bit cold", I answered, "I don't think the heater's turned up high enough."

Come to discover, we didn't have the damn thing turned on. Duh. Hey, we're from California. Neither of us have had occasion to use one of these kinds of heaters before. Besides, they said it was all automatic.

Although the weather outside wasn't frightful, inside it was nevertheless delightful with all the goings on of a traditional Christmas. There were aunts, uncles, cousins, gifts, football on TV, wood burning in the fireplace, lots of food, drink and spirited libations, many tall tales, merriment, and rejoicing. I felt genuinely privileged to have been included in their festivities and repeatedly expressed my gratitude.

About the football on TV that day, I'm not a sports fan at all but my friend Keith who is a fan noted that UCLA was in the Aloha Bowl on that day and, now hall of famer, Troy Aikman was quarterbacking for UCLA back then. For all I know, Eric's family may have been watching that game.

Anyway, after all the festivities, I staggered upstairs to bed. Turning on the heater was at the forefront of my mind, my number one mission. When I entered the attic, I zeroed in on my objective and executed my plan. It was warming up. I said to Jay, "Hopefully we won't be cold tonight."

We weren't.

* * *

Stirring awake the next morning feeling all comfy, I thought to myself, 'Hmm, it's kinda nice.'

Yup, the heater did its job. Jay and I were well rested and ready for the day. We got our things packed, tidied up the cots and blankets, then came downstairs with our bags. Eric wasn't up yet. Billy was making breakfast.

"Good mornin' boys. Hope y'all'er hungry."

Once again, I couldn't help but be a smartass, "Good mornin'. Hope you made enough", I said with a smile. Back then I had an enormous appetite. At a diner, I used to be able to kill off two full meals from the menu or a large serving platter of pasta with sauce and lots of parmesan cheese intended to feed four people. Can't do that anymore.

We joined Eric's dad who was at the table drinking a cup of coffee while reading the newspaper.

"Mornin' Rick".

He set down his paper, picked up his cup, looked over and reciprocated, "Mornin'," then took a sip.

With all the Christmas related activities and whatnot, Rick and I hadn't had much time to shoot the breeze until now.

"Mind if I ask how civilian life's been treatin' you so far?"

"Well, we just got here a couple of days before y'all arrived so I haven't had any time to think about it."

He took another sip of his coffee then remarked, "I see y'all's bags over by the door. Y'all leavin' already?"

"We kinda wanna get an early start seein's how we got almost 700 miles to go to Jay's grandma's house. But we won't leave before Eric's up or before breakfast, whichever comes later."

"Knowin' Eric, it'll be later. By the way, that was a nice surprise for Eric, y'all showin' up for Christmas and all." Looking at Jay, he said, "Hope everything works out for ya."

"Me too, sir. Thanks."

Just then, Billy, who joined us at the table, brought plates loaded with all manner of home cooked breakfast goodies. Billy enjoyed chitchat and asked, "So Mark, when do you need to be back at college?"

"The first day of spring quarter classes is January 4th. I kinda wanna be back on campus the Saturday before, so, the 2nd."

"That's just a week away. And you still need to get to Indiana before you can head back, right. Think you'll have enough time?"

"I think so. I mean, as long as I make it back to campus by Sunday afternoon, I'll be fine."

Eric had come down and joined us for breakfast at the table. Prompted, no doubt, by the bags next to the front door, he asked in a concerned tone, "Are you guys leavin' already?"

"Yeah we are. Like that Smokey and the Bandit song, *We Got a Long Way to Go and a Short Time to Get There*, we gotta get to Indiana before I can make my way back home. Then, I still hafta get down to UCLA before next Saturday."

"Aw, man, y'all just *got* here."

Jay and I were on our second helping of eggs, pancakes... "It's not like we're leavin' this second, dude, we gotta finish breakfast and brush our teeth 'n' sh... stuff." Almost slipped there.

We made such pigs of ourselves that by the time we were done eating, we could barely move, let alone carry our bags to the car and drive off.

"Well, Eric, we're gonna be stickin' around at least until we can move again." Calling out to his grandmother, I said, "Ms. Billy, you make a great breakfast."

* * *

Eric helped carry our bags out to the Firebird. It was cold and partially cloudy. We went back inside long enough to once again express our thanks, say goodbye and bid farewell to everyone. Eric came back outside and stood next to the car with us.

"Man, I'm really gonna miss you guys 'n' shit", he said.

119

"Right back atcha. Catch ya later, man."

"Later days, better lays", he said with a smile.

And with that, Jay, driving, and I got into the Firebird, rolled down the windows, put on the Megadeth tape full blast, then rolled westbound down the street toward 6th. I looked back one final time just as we turned left and saw Eric still on the sidewalk watching us drive away. I gave him one last goodbye wave before the house on the corner blocked my view.

I turned down the stereo and we rolled up the windows at the intersection of U.S. 24. There was no direct route back to interstate 70 so I told Jay to keep going straight till we got to K.S. 18 where we'd be heading east. From there we made a right onto Mink Rd. which took us all the way to I-70 where we took the east bound onramp.

"I like Eric 'n' all but I'm glad to be gettin' the hell outta that town", Jay said.

"I know whatcha mean 'n' shit. Good thing for Eric he's a 'really good friend'. But I kinda feel bad for him cuz he's stuck there."

"Yeah he is. If me and him had won the lotto, we woulda stayed in California. His dad woulda let him live with me. Shit, man, we woulda built a garage with a lift and all the stuff you need to fix up our cars 'n' shit ..."

He paused to reflect for a moment, let out a deep sigh then asked, "So, do I need to turn here?"

Dust in the Wind

After we got on I-70, I saw one of those signs that indicate how far the next few towns were and one of the upcoming towns was Topeka which is where the band Kansas originated which reminded me of their song, *Dust in the Wind*. We had spent more time in the State of Kansas than in all the other states we'd been in combined so far on this trip. We were also certain that we made a lasting impression on all those whom we had met, but, not to get all metaphysical and stuff, when all is said and done, we're all just "dust in the wind..."

The weather turned colder and some light snow started coming down. We were doing fine until we got to the other side of Topeka where I-70 merged with, and became, the Kansas Turnpike, a toll road.

For those of you who have never been on a turnpike, consider yourselves fortunate. Back in 1987, our highways and interstates in California were called freeways because they're free. I had heard of turnpikes — like the Jersey Turnpike — but thought they were a uniquely New England phenomenon. The deal with turnpikes, also known as controlled-access highways, is once you're on it, you're at its mercy. You don't pay to use it until you exit it. For the convenience of motorists, they have what are called "service areas" — like rest areas that include gas stations, restaurants, automotive repair, and sometimes even motels — located along the turnpike which are integrated with it. That means you don't actually exit the turnpike to access a service area, for doing so would cost you. Unfortunately, everything at the service area is more expensive than everywhere else off the turnpike but not so much more expensive so as to make it worth your while to pay to exit, get gas and a meal, then come back on. The out of pocket expenses of doing one over the other seem to favor exiting but the hassle factor of getting off, searching for services, then getting back on the turnpike is what tips the scale. Talk about a racket, they really got travelers by the balls. I never understood why the Jersey Turnpike was so berated in movies or TV shows until I had this experience with Jay. As you'll see, we had to endure this all the way into Kansas City.

As we approached the toll booth, we, being ignorant as we were, figured this may be some sort of agricultural checkpoint like we have in California. Nope. There was an arm-type gate like for a parking lot blocking the lane. We had to get a ticket so the gate would raise and we could continue our journey. The only tolls we had in California were for a few bridges like some in Frisco and one that connected Long

Beach to San Pedro. For those, we paid before crossing. Having to take a ticket was new for us.

I said to Jay, "Hey man, let me check out that ticket", so I could read it while he continued driving.

When I came upon the word "turnpike" I said, "Dude, I think we're on some kinda a toll road."

"How much?"

"This ticket doesn't have *any* useful information on it, so I have no idea. Let's see about takin' the next exit. Maybe I can learn somethin' there."

The next exit was a service area. I couldn't help but notice the gas prices, "*Dang*, dude, they're kinda proud of their gas 'n' shit."

We parked then went inside to learn about what we got ourselves into. We couldn't help but notice that pretty much everything was more expensive. We finally found a chart explaining the toll rates along with some motorist information. They also had the information in a pamphlet format so, of course, I grabbed one and studied it. The strategy session with Jay went something like this:

"Alright. Looks like we pretty much have two choices; stay on the turnpike and pay about $3.50, or get off the next exit where we pay a buck and change then go a different route. The advantages with the turnpike are; it's more direct, the services take Discover, and since it's a major roadway, they're more likely to keep it cleared of snow 'n' shit. According to the maps, goin' another route would add about 50 miles and there's no guarantee the businesses will accept Discover or the roads will even be clear if it snows any heavier. The choice is yours."

"Let's just stay on the turnpike."

"Good choice. By the way, we better not lose this ticket. They only accept cash and if we don't have the ticket, they'll charge us the full price which is $15.00", about $36.50 in today's money.

And, with that, we went back to the Firebird, topped off the tank, got inside, and sped off eastbound on the Kansas turnpike while the recently released *Welcome to The Jungle* by Guns N' Roses was playing on the radio.

* * *

Just beyond Kansas City, MO, we started seeing signs for year-round factory direct fireworks sales to the public. I said to Jay, "Hey, man, check it out. Fireworks factory selling direct to the public 'n' shit."

"Let's go check it out", he replied.

We went to the first place we saw and pulled into their parking lot. There was snow on the ground and it was a bit slippery but Jay managed to maintain control. The only building that was there looked like a large steel garage that was about the size of a triple-wide mobile home. 'Ok', I thought, 'but where's the factory?'

They had all sorts of stuff that would land you in all sorts of trouble in California so we were like a couple of kids in a candy store with no parents around.

Furthermore, being from California, I didn't understand how they could sell fireworks all year long so I asked them about that.

"We only sell fireworks to non-residents. The only time we can sell to Missouri residents is just before the 4th of July."

Unfortunately, they didn't take Discover so Jay and I had to be prudent with our purchases. In retrospect, that may have been a blessing in disguise. We got some of those Ground Bloom Flowers, firecrackers, and some colored smoke bombs that were the size of walnuts. Couldn't afford anything cool like mortars or Roman Candles. Oh well, perhaps some other time.

Rather than put the fireworks in the leaky trunk where they might get wet, we put them in the backseat, got back in the car, and continued our journey east. It wasn't more than maybe an hour later that we started feeling restless. You probably already guessed that something was about to happen.

We were still on the Missouri side as we were making our way through the city of St. Louis at around 70 mph, when we were seized by a mischievous streak. Jay was driving and asked, "Yo Mark, can you get me one of those smoke bombs?"

"Yeah I can."

I reached into the backseat for the bag of fireworks and brought it into the front between my legs. I opened a pack of smoke bombs and handed him one. He pushed the cigarette lighter all the way into its socket to energize it. When it popped out, he pulled it from its socket, lit the smoke bomb...

"Dude, what're you doin'?" I asked as he then shoved the smoke bomb into the ash tray and tried to close it.

"Damn it! It's not closing!" Jay exclaimed.

Before I had a chance to pull the smoke bomb out of the ashtray and toss it out the window, the entire cabin suddenly filled with purple smoke.

"*Fuck*, man, I can't see!"

Snow was still coming down when he did this and we had to roll down the windows and stick our heads outside just to see the road. Fortunately, the smoke dissipated fairly quickly but the fireworks smell, now mingled with stale cigarette smoke, lingered for another day or so.

"Fuck, dude, what the *hell* were you thinkin'?"

Jay responded, "I just wanted to see what it would do. I didn't think it was too big to close the ashtray and I didn't think it would make *that* much smoke 'n' shit."

"We could've crashed, man!" A few moments later I said, "It was kinda cool, though."

"How 'bout we toss one out the window and see what happens?" he suggested.

"With you goin' 80 miles an hour, we'd probably be too far down the road to see anything by the time it would start smokin' 'n' shit. But... if we tossed one into the bed of a pickup, we could watch and see if the driver notices it and what he does."

This just went from bad to worse. George Thorogood's *Bad to the Bone* must have been playing on the radio. I mean, messing with motorists at night the way we did in Texas was one thing but it was another thing entirely thinking that this current plan of throwing a lit pyrotechnic device into another motorist's moving vehicle while driving down a wet interstate at about 60 mph could not possibly go wrong... We did not for one moment consider any possible consequences to ourselves, let alone what could've happened to the targeted motorist or the other motorists around him.

So, it wasn't long before we spotted our victim. I grabbed a smoke bomb; this time, it was green. I pushed in the Firebird's cigarette lighter so it would heat up. Just when it popped out, Jay came up alongside the pickup, I rolled down the window and lit the smoke bomb then tossed it into the truck's bed.

"I think I got it in the bed", I said as I rolled the window back up.

Then, sure enough, smoke started billowing out the bed and I noticed the pickup's driver quickly turning his head both ways, looking over his shoulders.

"Dude! It's smokin' and the guy's checkin' it out 'n' shit! Let's go, *let's go*!!"

We took off figuring we didn't want to be around if this guy lost control. The guy didn't crash or anything but I'm sure he was royally pissed. Jay was quickly dashing between cars so as to get as much distance as possible as fast as possible between us and the pickup. It seemed like only a few minutes went by when Jay noticed a cop car with its lights on right behind us. Dare I say, cue *Breaking the Law* by Judas Priest?

"Oh *shit*, dude! I wonder if he's after *us*?"

For an instant, I thought Jay was going to try and out run him. I suggested, "Just go into the slow lane and see what he does."

As we went into the slow lane, the cop did the same, right behind us. Jay decided to pull completely over and the cop pulled over right behind us. Yes sirree, it was us he wanted as his next customer.

"Oh man", I lamented, "I'll betcha he saw what we did to that pickup."

When you're a heretical firebrand like we were, you fear getting busted in the here and now way more than tarnishing your soul for the hereafter but you still pray, "Oh God, *please* get me out of this".

We kept our cool and the cop came up to the passenger side, my side. I rolled down the window and the cop said, "Driver, please get your license and registration and meet me back at my patrol car."

I noticed he had "Illinois" on his badge and patches. We didn't notice the Gateway Arch when we crossed the state line from Missouri into Illinois. Then again, the weather was a bit foul and we were kinda preoccupied with doing stupid shit so it's not hard to believe we didn't see it.

Jay did as the officer instructed and commented to me, "Hope this doesn't take too long 'n' shit."

He stepped out of the Firebird, closed the door, walked back to the passenger side of the patrol car, opened that door, stepped in then closed the door. Jay had less love for the boys in blue than I, and I had practically none. Shortsighted assholes like us saw them as goose-stepping jackbooted thugs who abused their authority and had nothing better to do than break up our house parties, hand out traffic tickets, and do all sorts of things to keep us from having fun. So, after what seemed like 15 minutes, Jay came back to the Firebird and I asked, "Why did he stop us? What happened?"

"He said I was speeding and he's got my license and registration, and now I gotta follow him to the police station 'n' shit."

"What for?"

"Because I'm from out of state, I'm gonna hafta post bail right now or else stay in jail 'til the trial."

"WHAT?!"

* * *

In my experience, highway patrol or state troopers zero in on out-of-state motorists more than residents. I suspect they do that because non-residents tend to be ignorant of lesser known local laws such as making a right turn while a pedestrian is standing on the sidewalk of said corner. That's a real thing. The legal supposition is the pedestrian, who has the right of way, may be intending to cross a street. Anyway, when a non-resident gets popped for a traffic violation, they are less likely to pay it when they get home, especially if they're moving from one state to another, as was the case with Jay. So, they extort immediate payment of bail under threat of incarceration. Furthermore, a non-resident is far less likely to appear in court in order to fight the ticket which financially benefits the jurisdiction in the form of forfeited bail. Yet another total money-making racket.

Jay started up the Firebird and the cop pulled out off the shoulder with us right behind him. I could tell from the look on Jay's face that he was thinking about running and I couldn't blame him.

"I know what you're thinkin' 'n' shit, but I *wouldn't* if I were you. We *just* crossed into Illinois and we still gotta cross the *whole* state before we get into Indiana. This cop's a state trooper and his jurisdiction is *the entire state* 'n' shit. His radio can go infinitely faster than the Firebird. Remember rule number 1."

I suddenly had a horrific thought which I shared with Jay, "Wait a minute... You said he's got your registration 'n' shit?"

"Yeah he does."

"But your dad's name is on the registration, right?"

Jay's eyes opened wide.

"Do you still have your military ID to show you're his dependent 'n' shit?"

"Yeah, I'm pretty sure I do."

"Ok. I hope that'll be enough so they don't call 'em."

"What if they call?"

"I don't know, man. Probably end of the line 'n' shit."

Wouldn't that be a kick in the teeth? To come *this far* only to be stopped dead in our tracks. I can imagine it now... Jay's dad gets a call from an Illinois state trooper asking, "Hello Sir. Do you have a son?"

The fallout in the wake of the shit storm caused by that call would be monumentally epic.

* * *

The officer led us to a parking lot where Jay parked the Firebird then handed me the keys saying, "Just in case."

Jay and I both stepped out and I asked the officer to explain what was happening.

He said, "He's gonna be processed and will hafta post bail or stay in jail 'til the trial."

"Can I come along in case he needs something?"

"No one allowed but authorized personnel unless you're his lawyer?" he asked.

"I'm not. So, how long will this take?"

"If he posts bail, it shouldn't take long."

131

He escorted Jay from the parking lot to the building where I watched a door open, they stepped inside, then the door closed. The building was made of lots of concrete painted grey and didn't appear to have any windows. It looked bleak and imposing like a fortress. I went back to the Firebird, sat inside, closed the door, and waited. The snow had let up. About a half hour went by and I was starting to feel a bit of a chill; it was pretty cold outside. After another half hour, I wondered if there was a lobby area inside where I could wait. I was thinking to myself, 'The guy said it wouldn't take long. I wonder what he meant by "not long"? Maybe he just straight up lied to me, he is a cop, after all, and they lie all the time.'

More time went by and I got so cold that I started the car just to run the heater. The weather was overcast and a few flakes of snow were falling again. After I got all warmed up, I shut off the car and waited some more. It was probably an hour and a half after we first parked when I got out of the car, walked across the parking lot and cautiously went up to the door. I cautiously pulled on it to see if it would open... nope, it's solid. No knob or lever to operate a latching mechanism. I was then suddenly startled by an amplified voice blaring at me over a PA, "WHAT IS IT YOU WANT?!"

I looked around and spotted a CCTV camera pointed at the door. I looked into the camera and answered, "I'm waiting for a friend of mine to be finished processing and I was wondering if you had a lobby or a waiting area where I could wait for him until he's done! It's pretty cold out here!"

Whoever was at the other end of the PA speaker was a heartless automaton devoid of any shred of humanity or compassion, "THERE'S NO PLACE FOR YOU TO WAIT INSIDE THE DETENTION CENTER!"

"Well, do you know how much longer before Jay's released?"

No reply.

"Hello?!"

Still no reply. With law enforcement personnel displaying such disdain to someone who's asking valid questions, it's no wonder they're not shown any compassion, let alone respect. What comes around goes around — karma.

Finally, "VACATE THE PREMISES OR YOU'LL BE ARRESTED!"

And here I thought Jay and I were dicks. The main difference between us and this guy was he had a badge and a gun. As much as I wanted to flip the middle finger into the camera lens and say to him, 'YOU ARE WHAT YOU EAT, YOU DICK!', I resisted.

I turned around, went back across the parking lot to the Firebird, got in, then waited some more. It got to the point where I started formulating alternate courses of action, that is, what I would do if Jay had to stay the night or longer. How would I even get in touch with Jay to let him know what I was doing?

That compound didn't appear to have a front desk, let alone a lobby. And the guy on the other end of the CCTV camera was about as useful as an anvil to someone who's drowning. So, I waited some more.

* * *

It seems like nearly three hours went by before Jay finally emerged from the detention center, to my great delight, of course. He walked across the parking lot at a brisk pace, came up to the Firebird, got in, then slammed the door.

"Fuckin' *assholes*!"

He started the car and I asked, "What happened dude?"

He was pretty pissed and almost peeled out of the parking lot as we left while *Wild Side* by Mötley Crüe was playing. "Those mother fuckers were takin' their sweet fuckin' time gettin' the fuckin' paperwork ready 'n' shit. God damn fuckin' pigs sittin' on their fat asses stuffin' their fat faces with donuts. They were tryin' to scare me tellin' me how they got a nice cell for me with a couple of cellmates where I'd be stayin' till the trial. Sayin' shit like, 'You a long way from California boy' and 'Out here, we teach folks to have respect for the law, not like they do in la la land.' They were thinkin' I couldn't afford the bail but they were surprised when I slapped the $87.00 (about $212.00 today) down on the table and said, 'Can I fuckin' go now?' Fuckin' cock suckers didn't expect that."

Well, you get the idea. Jay continued to vent as we got back onto the interstate. We continued straight on through the State of Illinois to Terre Haute, just on the other side of the Illinois – Indiana state line, where we fueled up.

"Alright," I said as we got back into the Firebird, "Only about a hundred more miles to go. It should be downhill from here."

Off to Grandma's House We Go

We were in the home stretch, the final leg of our journey to Jay's grandmother's place. To be specific, Jay's final leg. I still needed to get back home then to UCLA. It was nighttime that Saturday, December 26, and I only had a week to get back to school.

Before we got to the outskirts of the city, I noticed a White Castle on the other side of the interstate and muttered to myself, "Ooo, a White Castle."

Jay quickly asked, "What?"

"Oh, nothin', just a White Castle."

"Where?" he asked anxiously looking around.

"On the other side of the freeway, we just passed it."

Jay took the very next exit, crossed over the underpass, then headed back the opposite direction via the side road whence we gradually came upon the White Castle burger place and parked in its parking lot. I had never been to a White Castle before so this would be a new experience for me. I don't remember if Jay had ever been to one before this but he sure was excited to eat there. We looked over the menu then placed our order. When I've mentioned this part of the story to people, I get either a "love it" or "hate it" reaction to White Castle. It seems most folks are kinda polar about it. Personally, I'm indifferent. I've had better but it's far from the worst I've had. I don't remember anything else about that visit other than we ordered a lot of food, ate all of it, liked it, got back in the Firebird and continued our journey with no ill after effects.

* * *

We were approaching Indianapolis and we were, once again, feeling a bit restless. Now was as good as time as any to stop off at a gas station, top off the tank and get a local map so as to find exactly where grandma lived. We exited in what I can only describe as a sketchy part of town. Even though it was nighttime, we could see graffiti illuminated by street lights, a few homeless guys sleeping in doorways, littered streets, and a couple abandoned storefronts.

Jay spoke up, "Hey, man. How about we light a pack of firecrackers and toss it at one of those homeless dudes?"

I cracked a mischievous smile, nodded in agreement and added, "What say we do it after we gas up 'n' shit. You know, like on our way back to the freeway so we can make a clean getaway."

Jay nodded and said, "Ok."

We got the gas and a map then set out to wreak havoc. We went back along the same route we used to get to the gas station and it took us no time at all to find a homeless guy sleeping next to a storefront. I got a pack of firecrackers from our stash, rolled down the window, lit the firecrackers then tossed them at the sleeping homeless guy. We started slowly rolling away when the firecrackers started going off. That homeless guy totally freaked out and panicked like there was a drive-by happening right then and there. Jay floored the accelerator and headed straight for the freeway. Man, we sure did a lot of really shitty stuff.

So, Jay's grandmother lived on the other side of Indianapolis in Greenfield. Jay informed me that his grandmother had a heart condition and he didn't want to startle her, shock her, surprise her, or in any other way cause her to become over excited.

"No problem, man, I totally understand 'n' shit." I then asked him, "Whaddya have in mind?"

"I think we should look for a motel room for tonight then I'll call her sometime tomorrow."

"Ok, sounds good."

We found a nondescript motel, got a room and settled in for the night. Jay was understandably apprehensive. He was practically at the end of his journey, the finish line was in sight. He was on the threshold of the next chapter of his life and he had more hopes than expectations. His life was completely turned upside-down just one week earlier and he's been in a state of flux since. Life on the road doesn't really allow one too much time to reflect on the state of one's life. I mean, yeah, sure there are long stretches of road where you're just keeping the car within the

lane but the act of keeping the car on the road suffi-
ciently occupies the mind to prevent one from completely focusing on the current state of the universe
and one's role within it. Jay's disposition caused me to
experience some trepidation. After laying out all that
cash for bail, I didn't know if he'd have enough to
send me home. Oh well, nothing to be done about it
and no amount of worrying will change that. It was
time to hit the sack.

* * *

It sure was nice to sleep in and it looked like Jay
was still sleeping in. I got up, took a shower, got
dressed, then started studying the local maps we got
the previous night. The grandmother's address was
easy to find and I plotted a simple route to get us
there.

Jay was stirring so I asked him, "Hey, man, you
gonna get up anytime soon? I'm jonesin' for some
breakfast 'n' shit."

He kinda rolled over and groaned then asked,
"What time is it?"

The smartass in me answered, "Breakfast time.
There's *bound* to be some good eats around here."

Still lethargic from just waking up, he mustered
up about as much enthusiasm as a third grader trying
to get ready for school on a chilly, rainy Monday
morning. I started to think he was more conflicted
than he originally let on. Although he was eager to get

here, he was also anxious about meeting his grand-mother.

He got up and went into the bathroom to shit, shower, and shave. I think I turned on the TV to find some news while I waited. Check out time for the motel was 11:00 o'clock in the morning and that time was quickly approaching... and I was getting hangry.

"*Come on*, man, we gotta check out by eleven or we'll be charged for another day 'n' shit. Besides, I'm starvin'!"

Jay eventually got with it, we packed our stuff into the Firebird, then headed out for brunch to someplace I can't recall. While we were there, I asked Jay, "When're you gonna call your grandmother?"

"Since it's Sunday, she'll be at church 'n' shit so, maybe around 1:00 o'clock. We can wash my car after we eat."

Yup, Jay was avoiding calling his grandmother. Or, he's at least putting it off for as long as he can. I had never known Jay to be nervous or hesitant about anything which really concerned me. Meanwhile, I was getting increasingly anxious myself but for reasons which were different than Jay's.

After our meal, we asked the waitress where the nearest car wash was. She looked at us a bit oddly and said, "There's one over on State St. but I don't think they're open."

It was Sunday and winter, so it did seem like a bit of wishful thinking that it would be open. But, we went there anyway and discovered that it was, indeed, closed. The sky was overcast and the ground was somewhat dry with puddles here and there, and in areas that were shaded from the sun, there were scattered patches of snow. The car wash had a payphone so I said to Jay, "Hey, man, now's a good a time as any to call your grandma 'n' shit."

He hesitated for a bit and looked rather nervous. I then calmly said, "Look, it's obvious you're tryin' to put off callin' her 'n' shit. Can you level with me and tell me why?"

He took a deep breath then let out a long sigh and confessed, "I don't *really* know if she'll let me live with her."

Whoa, didn't see that coming. He went on, "The last time I talked with her I said how I'd like to move to Indiana and she said, 'That'd be nice'. I mean, do *you* think she's okay with me moving in with her?"

My first thought was that the premise to get me to go along on this trip was a lie. Needless to say, I was pretty pissed.

"You mean you decided to come all the way out here without knowing fer sure that you'd be able to stay? And you're only *now* telling me about this?"

Jay's behavior completely made sense in the wake of this revelation. Him not knowing what his grandmother would think about him being here had been weighing on his mind since he decided to make this trek, and the weight of that uncertainty got heavier with every mile. Add to that the matter of betraying my trust.

"I didn't think about it like that. I mean, I didn't mean to lie to you. I mean, I didn't really lie. What I meant is I've been thinkin' about how I was gonna tell you. I thought I could figure everything out before we got here. And as we got closer I was thinkin', 'shit, we're really doin' this.' I couldn't believe we really did this. I mean, I been wantin' to visit Leanne and then we did, but then there was *Christmas* with *Eric* and now we're actually *here*."

He paused for a moment, took another deep breath, then said, "I really liked bein' on the road with you and..."

He again paused for just a moment then said, "...I kinda didn't want it to end."

After one more pause, he said, "I'm so sorry, Mark."

This admission was the hardest thing I've ever seen Jay do. This was a pivotal moment. Up until now, he had been betrayed and disappointed by so many people in his life that he figured the only person he could really count on was himself. I felt bad, not only for him, but because I had misunderstood him the way most teenagers who act out are misunderstood.

I looked him in the eye and said, "Dude, you asked me to come along as your mechanic. I *agreed* to come along because I'm your *friend*. I made you a promise to help you get to your grandma's place and I mean to *keep* that promise, even if I hafta *beat* your ass into the *trunk* of this car and drive you there the rest of the way *myself*. Now, are you gonna call your grandma or what?"

He said, "Alright. Gotta be careful to not give her a heart attack."

We walked up to the phone, Jay lifted the handset, put in a quarter, started to dial then hung up. "Forgot I don't need the area code 'n' shit."

He lifted the handset again, retrieved the quarter from the coin return slot, put it back into the phone, and dialed the number. "It's ringin'…" he said. "Hello, gran, this is Jay."

I could barely hear what sounded like a woman speaking energetically on the other end. All I could hear clearly was Jay's side of the conversation which went something like this.

"Yeah, it's really me, I'm o… yes, I'm fine. Well, that's what I'm callin' you about. I couldn't stay at home anymore so I *had* to leave. Well, I would like to come see you. No. No, *please* don't call my parents until I see you. Yeah, I'll tell you all about it when I see you. Really? Are you sure? It won't take me long at all. I'm in Indiana right now. I can be there in about ten minutes and I'm bringin' a friend with me. Grandma? You ok? Yeah, I'm just a few minutes away. Ok. See you soon."

Jay hung up the phone, turned toward me and said, "I guess we're all set to see my grandma 'n' shit. Let's go."

We got back in the Firebird. Jay started it up as I opened the map to navigate. I then said, "Ok, go down this street and turn left at the light."

* * *

It was a short drive to grandma's place and *Spirit of the Radio* by Rush was playing. Seeing how that song is upbeat, I was hoping it would help lighten the mood. Jay was more obedient of the traffic laws in those last few miles than he'd been at any other time during the entire trip. This impending meeting with his grandmother was really affecting him. I was wondering if Jay was still keeping yet another worry to himself.

As we rounded the corner onto the street where his grandmother's place was, I said, "According to the house numbers, it looks like it's just a few houses down on the right-hand side."

Jay was slowly easing the Firebird down the street.

"Hold on for a sec...", I said to examine the house numbers. "Go to the next house... There it is!"

Jay stopped long enough to look over the house then pulled into the driveway.

"Well, we're here."

We stepped out of the Firebird, went up to the front door and knocked. It didn't dawn on me yet that this was the last time I would ever ride in Jay's Firebird.

An older chick who I could only assume was Jay's grandmother answered the door. Her face lit up and Jay couldn't help but crack a smile. They hugged each other as they greeted one another. When they pulled back Jay said, "Gran, I wanna introduce you to my friend Mark."

"Mark, so nice to meet you. You boys come on in out of the cold and make yourselves at home." Directing her statements toward Jay, she said, "Your mother's called here every day askin' if I'd heard from you. I should call her and let her know you're ok."

"Grandma, please don't do that. At least not until I tell you what happened."

"She told me how you and your father had a fallin' out and she's been worried sick about you. She said all is forgiven and they just want you to be safe at home."

Jay's mother is the grandmother's daughter which explains why she wanted to call her about Jay's arrival so she wouldn't worry about him. I could tell that the grandmother's maternal instincts were obscuring her view of what sort of person her daughter really was, so, as much as I didn't — and still don't — want to get involved with a family's internal problems and struggles, I was compelled to interject.

"Excuse me, Ms..."

"Oh, please call me Mary"

"Very well. Mary, though I'm technically a non-related third-party, may I offer some insight?"

She responded with "Ok" in a tone that communicated, 'that's right, you're not a member of this family, so who do you think you are by getting involved.'

I said, "Jay asked me to come with him on this trip mainly as his mechanic but also as his friend. And as his friend, I am by default his advocate. And as such, I respectfully ask that you exercise some patience and indulge Jay in his need to tell you his side of the story before you make a call to his mother."

After a bit more pleading, she was convinced to hear Jay's side before calling. That was a very wise decision as you'll soon see.

Jay started by reminding Mary of the times he told her about things which had happened before he got the Firebird and how things got worse afterwards. He then gave her the low down on what led up to the incident in Salinas followed by a summary of the incident itself. I testified to the accuracy of what happened in Salinas. Mary was at once riveted with her eyes wide open and her mouth slightly agape, and awash in disbelief often shaking her head with her eyes closed. Now, mind you, Jay understandably left out many of the unsavory and unflattering details of his sojourn to salvation but he accurately relayed everything I was a direct witness to.

"I can't *believe* Alice would allow that to happen, let alone be part of it", Mary remarked about her daughter, Jay's mother.

"I wouldn't lie to you about somethin' this serious, grandma. That's why I had to come here."

Mary reflected for a moment then said, "I think I'm gonna hold off on callin' your mother for now but I will call your uncle Richard, the lawyer, have him come over here and see what he has to say."

She got Richard on the phone and briefed him on the situation. After she finished her conversation with him and hung up, she said, "He said he'll be here later this afternoon. Meanwhile, I'll fix us some snacks and refreshments then maybe we can talk about some more pleasant things."

"Do you need help with anything?"

"No thank you, not at all. Y'all just relax, after the adventure you've had."

When she entered the kitchen, I said to Jay, "So, how 'bout when she gets back, you talk to her about sendin' me back home?"

"Don't worry, man, I'll talk to her about it. Just, can't dump everything on her all at once. Gotta break it to her a little at a time 'n' shit."

Jay and I migrated over to the dining room table just as Mary came back in with food and drink.

"So, Mark, how'd you meet Jay?"

Ah, yes, seemingly idle chitchat. I decided to use this to my advantage to force the issue of my getting home.

"We were introduced by a mutual friend named Eric."

"Did y'all go to the same school?"

"No, I had graduated from a different high school a year before I met Eric, then Jay later on." This was where I made my move. "Right now, I'm enrolled at UCLA. Classes start back up on January 4th."

"UCLA? You mean in California?"

"Yes ma'am."

"How're you gonna get back?"

I turned toward Jay and gave him a stern look. Quickly realizing he was on the hot seat, he finally came clean. This was probably that "other worry" he was keeping to himself I mentioned earlier.

"I told him you'd help me pay for his ticket home."

I immediately followed up with, "You see, Mary, we had an agreement. Jay asked me for help the day after the car chase in Salinas. I listened to what he had to say and gave him advice whereupon he asked if I would go on this journey with him. I made it clear to him when I had to be back in school and he convinced me that one way or another, he would make sure that I would make it back on time."

Just then, Jay interjected, "I practically owe my life to Mark. I wouldn't've been able to make it here without him. He made sure I got here, now I hafta make sure he gets home. I'll sell my car to pay you back if I have to."

Mary was overcome with compassion and said to Jay, "That won't be necessary." Turning then to me, she said, "Don't worry, we'll get you home on time.

And thank you so much for helpin' my Jay Bird through all this."

I suddenly had a huge grin on my face, looked over at Jay and said, "Jay Bird?"

"Gran'ma!"

I couldn't help but giggle, "'Jay Bird'. Oh man..."

"Shut up or I'll kick your ass!"

"JAY!" Mary exclaimed, "Language."

Still giggling, I said, "Don't sweat it dude, it's not like you'll ever be goin' back to Fort Ord. Besides, it's not like I'm gonna track down everyone you know *just* to tell 'em that. Besides, it's way better than 'jail-bird'."

Yeah, we had a good laugh about that.

* * *

So, uncle Richard eventually arrived with his wife, greetings and introductions were exchanged, then we all got right down to the matter at hand; Jay's arrival and everything that it entailed. I don't remember the exact time but I do remember it had been nighttime for a while. It was probably five or six o'clock.

Richard was fully briefed and asked some questions regarding the Firebird's title and registration as well as the Discover card and what purchases were made on it. I also briefed him about my friend Mario and his lawyer brothers in case he wanted to consult them regarding California law.

Mary anxiously stated, "I *really* should call Alice to let her know Jay's here."

Richard said, "I think it's okay to call her now. There's no damage to the car, the credit card bill shouldn't be too outrageous, and, of course, Jay's ok. There's no reason to be concerned about the ticket he got in St. Louis since it sounds like it was all taken care of."

I could tell that Jay was borderline freaking out which made me a bit anxious for him. However, everyone had to put on a calm demeanor for Mary's benefit.

Mary dialed the phone to call Alice, her daughter, Jay's mother. Alice answered.

"Hello, Alice? This is Mary. Well, I'm callin' because I have news about Jay. He just showed up here out of the blue and is with me right now. Yes, that's right and... well the car's here too; he drove it here... Now, now, there's no reason for you to get so upset. Jay's ok, the car's ok... hello? *Hello*? ... I think she hung up."

Mary was beside herself. Jay was frozen. Richard and his wife stared at each other with a look of "what just happened" on their faces.

Mary said, "I've never seen her act this way. She was *so* angry I couldn't get a word in edgewise. She seemed to be more mad than relieved that Jay was here and that he and the car were ok."

Richard said, "Yeah, mom, that's pretty weird. I mean, she and Bruce haven't always treated Jay as well as they should..."

Mary interrupted with, "They're *doin'* the best they can. Should I call her back?" almost as though she were seeking a consensus.

Richard then went on with, "Nevertheless, mom, as angry as she is, I don't think callin' her back would be wise. It may be best to let her cool off. She now knows Jay is here and she'll probably call back when she's ready."

"Oh, I hope so", Mary said.

Richard quickly changed the subject. Looking at us he asked, "You guys look hungry. What say we order some pizzas?"

I was never one to pass on an opportunity for some grub, "Oh man, some 'za sounds great right about now. Order mine with as much meat as can be put on it."

Richard's wife phoned the order in. Meanwhile, we all sat around the table rehashing Jay's home life, the factors that influenced his decision to make this journey and, most importantly to me, my return trip. Richard took the lead on that.

"We gotta see about gettin' you back to school in time for the start of class, right?"

"Right. I actually gotta get back home to Fort Ord first then from there I can make my way down to UCLA."

"I see. So by when do you need to be home?"

"Ideally, the sooner, the better. I was home for only one week before I embarked on this trip with Jay, so, I couldn't spend Christmas with my mother."

The doorbell rang; it was the pizza guy. Jay and I brought the pizzas in and placed them on the dining table while Richard paid the driver. Richard's wife and Mary brought plates, flatware and drinks from the kitchen. I always wondered about that; plates and flatware for pizza, that is. I mean, ok, plates, maybe, but flatware? Who uses a fork and a knife to eat pizza?

"Alright! Let's *eat*. Go on, dig in."

To young firebrands like Jay and me, pizza was the perfect food combining the four food groups: meat, dairy (the cheese), cereals & grains (the crust), and fruits & vegetables (tomatoes, onions, etc.). We hadn't had pizza the entire trip so this was a real bonanza for us.

While feasting on all this glorious za, I noticed red and blue lights flashing outside through the closed window curtains, my adrenalin started surging, heartrate went up, respiration went up, alert level went up — I thought to myself, 'those are police lights'.

* * *

Mary lived in a nice, respectable suburban neighborhood that was very much a bedroom community. Nothing ever happens there to warrant a special visit by the local police. Seeing flashing red and blue lights was an attention getter for the neighbors and a serious concern for Mary's family. This was likely to upset her so we all kept our cool. But, the cops had other intentions.

As we all looked at each other around the table, some of us with our mouths full of pizza, cheese dangling from our bottom lip, we heard come over the police PA, "EVERYONE INSIDE THE HOUSE! COME OUT WITH YOUR HANDS UP! WE HAVE YOU SURROUNDED!"

That's right. *Holy fucking shit*! What the *fuck* was going on?

"COME OUT WITH YOUR HANDS UP AND NO ONE WILL GET HURT!"

Richard & his wife, Jay, and I tried to play down the situation so as to not upset Mary, with negligible success. She was getting anxious and looking like she was about to have a cardiac episode.

"What's goin' on? Are they in front of *my* house? Do they mean *us*?"

Richard, being the lawyer, took the initiative and stood up then said, "I'm sure it's ok, mom. I'll just go and take a look to see if their focus is on us."

Moving a window curtain just enough to see out to the street, he said, "I see about a dozen cop cars outside. It looks like they are talkin' about us. There must be some sort of mistake. I'll go out and have a chat with them and find out what's goin' on. Meanwhile, the rest of you can go ahead and finish eating."

'Oh thank god', I thought. 'It would be a crime to let all this pizza go to waste and worse, it would suck to go to jail hungry.'

He took off his jacket so the cops could see he had nothing concealed, and he held it in his hand — it was pretty cold outside — then slowly opened the door and went outside to speak with the officers.

While grabbing another slice of pizza, I tried to recall what all Jay and I may have done since we drove into this State that would've pissed off the cops this much. 'Could it have been the firecrackers we threw at that sleeping homeless guy? Seems a bit extreme since it was just firecrackers.'

Tense situations like these always seem to take longer than they really do so please bear with me. After maybe 20 minutes, the cops turned off the lights. Less than 10 minutes after that, Richard came back into the house with quite the story to tell but first, Mary asked him, "Do I need to go out there and talk to them?"

"No, mother. Everything's under control. It was all just a terrible misunderstanding. The sheriff said that his department received a phone call from what sounded like a panicked woman claimin' that there was a man at this address who was armed & dangerous, AWOL from the army, had stolen a red Firebird and was holdin' hostages within the residence."

Just over twenty years later, this type of call would come to be known as "SWATting" by the FBI then eventually entered into the Oxford dictionary in 2015.

Just for kicks, let's analyze how many lies were told in this call. Jay was not dangerous and the only thing he was armed with was an appetite for pizza. Jay was never in the army and you can't be AWOL without actually being in the army. The Firebird being stolen; well, in all fairness, per the letter of the law, the car was registered in Bruce's name and Jay didn't have permission to drive it, so, technically, it was stolen, but upon investigation, it was never reported as such. Holding hostages; Jay came to this residence not to seek hostages but to seek sanctuary from his parents' persecution. Interestingly, there was no mention of a stolen credit card.

Anyway, you can imagine just how dumbfounded we all must have looked.

Richard continued, "As for the extensive police response, the sheriff told me that just a couple of months ago, they had a deputy get shot, the first one in some thirty plus years, so they're a little hypersensitive when responding to an armed suspect call. Based on what the sheriff said, it sounds like it was Alice who placed that call."

Can you believe it? Jay's own mother made a call that could've resulted in the death of her own son and her own mother. Well, Mary couldn't believe it either.

"Alice would do somethin' like *this* to her own flesh and blood? This isn't the daughter *I* raised. She *can't* be my daughter..."

She continued to mutter on about that for a little longer. Even Richard, who wasn't blinded by sibling love, was genuinely shocked at what his sister had done. I shudder to think how this scenario would've played out had he not been there that night when the cops showed up. Every time I relive this part of the story, I'm still taken aback. Jay and I did our share of stupid shit because we were young guys suffering from testosterone poisoning. But there was no excuse for Jay's mother to have done what she did, and the only explanation I can think of is vengeful blind rage. Going back for a moment to when we were stopped by the cops in Illinois, imagine what would've happened had they called Bruce to confirm he was Jay's father.

Once the police had left and we had all calmed down from the near SWAT experience, the shape and tone of the conversation around the table changed drastically. Before this, Mary had been hoping for an amicable reunion or at least a peaceful meeting of the minds resulting in a mutual understanding where everyone would be singing "Kumbaya". This incident galvanized Mary and Richard's resolve to do whatever it took to help Jay with his life moving forward and, more importantly, help to get Jay's sister away from the toxic environment her parents created.

Richard was already formulating strategies to get Bruce to sign the title of the Firebird over to Jay. "By makin' that call to the sheriff, Alice committed the crime of filin' a false police report. If Bruce resists signin' the title over to you, I can use that call to help him see the light, let 'em know that in the eyes of the law, he could be considered a co-conspirator or an accomplice. We could also look into doin' a lien sale..."

This was all well and dandy but I was a bit more concerned with getting home. I wanted to resume discussion on that topic which was interrupted by the arrival of pizza followed by the cops.

After a while, Richard finished up with, "I think that covers it for now. Anything else?"

That's when I spoke up like Columbo, a 1970's TV detective whose catch phrase is, "Just one more thing."

"Right! You need to get home. I'll see to it personally first thing tomorrow morning. It's gettin' late and I can tell you that for me, the excitement of this evening has really worn on me."

Mary followed that with, "I'll get the guest room ready for you Mark, and Jay, I have another room you can stay in. Go get your things out of the car and make yourselves at home."

Ooo, a legit guest room rather than an unfinished attic. I was really looking forward to that. I didn't realize just how wiped I was until I laid down.

Oh man, what a day.

Homeward Bound

I don't know about you, but for me, the moment when I first wake up in a bed other than my own is frequently very disorienting. My first thought is usually, 'Where the f...', quickly followed by, 'oh, yeah, that's right.' My next thought is, 'I gotta pee'.

It was the morning of Monday, December 28. I had accomplished what I had set out to do in regards to my agreement with, and obligation to, Jay. And now, I really needed to be making my way back home. I got dressed and gathered my things together so as to be ready to go. It may have been around seven or eight o'clock in the morning. I walked down the hall into the kitchen where Mary was reading the paper and drinking a cup of coffee.

"Good mornin', Mark. Would you like a cup of coffee?"

"Good mornin'. Thank you, I would"

"How'd you sleep last night?"

"Quite well, thank you, especially after all the excitement from last night."

"Oh my lord, I know. I was up half the night thinkin' about it. I still can't believe Alice did that," shaking her head while she said that.

She then asked, "Would you like some breakfast?"

"I sure would, thank you."

You gotta love home-cooked mid-western comfort food; eggs, bacon, sausage, potatoes, pancakes...

"Richard should be here soon and he'll make sure you get back home."

"Thanks again, Mary. I'm glad everything worked out to where I was available to help Jay. The timing though was eerily coincidental that this whole thing went down while I'm on winter break from college. Maybe it was meant to be."

She thanked me profusely for keeping her Jaybird safe and lavished me with flattering praise and accolades which I'm too modest to repeat. I know, huh, me, modest? Well, although everyone appreciates acknowledgment and recognition for good deeds, many of us tend put on a bashful smile and respond along the lines of, "Aw, shucks, 'tweren't nothin', anyone woulda done the same." In my case, I would feel as though I were boasting which, as I said in my introduction, is incredibly narcissistic.

That stuff aside, Mary and I did chitchat about some other things like what Jay, our mutual friends and I did back home, my schooling, career plans, places my mom and I had been stationed at, etc.

Jay came in, "Mornin' all."

Mary and I reciprocated "Good mornin'" almost in unison.

While Mary was fixing Jay some breakfast and telling him about how she and I had a nice conversation, I was wondering when Richard was going to arrive.

Jay finished his breakfast then he and I helped Mary clear the table. She stayed in the kitchen to wash the dishes and Jay and I went into the living room to just hang for a bit.

Jay started right in, "Mark, man, thanks again for helpin' me come out here and I'm sorry for the shit that went down last night. My mom's *totally* fucked in the head. I mean, I know my parents are all whacked 'n' shit but to send the *cops* out here like that...that's just *way* beyond fucked up."

"Don't sweat it, man. The important thing is no one got shot and you're grandma's okay 'n' shit. Anyway, that's all in the past now. Time for you to start thinkin' about and figurin' out whatcha gonna do now that you're here. Couldn't hurt to go to college 'n' shit, at least a JC. I think you're grandma'd be willin' to help you with that."

"Yeah, man. Maybe. We'll hafta see."

"No worries, dude. As for me, I'm pretty much just waitin' for Richard to get here to take me to the airport."

"Are you thinkin' 'bout flyin' into San Francisco?"

"Maybe. Monterey has an airport but it's really small so I may need to change planes in Frisco."

"How're you gonna get home from the airport 'n' shit?"

"Monterey airport is practically across the street from Noah's house. I'll just call him to pick me up. That way, my mom won't be the wiser. When Noah drops me off, I'll just tell her I'm back from the retreat 'n' shit."

We continued to shoot the breeze until Richard came over which was probably around 9:00 o'clock.

He came in and said, "Mornin' boys."

"Mornin'"

"Ok, Mark, let's see about gettin' you home. Where exactly do you need to go?"

"Monterey, California."

"Would you know if they have a Greyhound station there?"

I didn't anticipate them sending me back on a bus. I've ridden on Greyhound busses before this. A lot of folks who utilize bus lines like Greyhound and Trailways tend to be eccentric and not usually in an entertaining way. I realize that labeling passengers on the national bus lines as eccentric seems hypocritical especially after my ride on a Green Tortoise bus, but the clientele who patronize the Green Tortoise tend to be college age hostellers, a demographic I could understand and relate to. The "weird" passengers on "regular" busses tend to suffer from mental illness. I can deal with stoners, I can't deal with psychos.

"Uh, no, I don't", I answered Richard.

"No problem, I can find out when I call to book your ticket. By the way, what's the next big city near Monterey?"

"Well, Salinas is about 15 miles away and San Francisco is just over a hundred."

I wasn't keen on taking a bus some 2000 miles but I didn't know how to breach this topic considering Jay and I showed up unannounced and they were sending me back on their dime. So, I had to make peace with whatever travel arrangements they were going to make for me.

"Got it", Richard said. "I'll go make the call right now."

I turned towards Jay and gave him a disapproving 'I'm going by bus?' kind of look. He came back with a look that said, 'Hey, man, I didn't know they'd send you back on a bus.' My eyes rolled and I sighed.

Richard got off the phone and relayed, "We're all set. Your bus leaves the station in downtown today just after 12:00 noon and you should arrive in Salinas the day after tomorrow at around 5:30 in the evening. You will need to change busses in San Francisco. I'll give you a ride to the station whenever you're ready."

* * *

Although I wasn't looking forward to spending the next two-and-a-half days with a busload of weirdos, at least Richard treated me better than my own relatives. Just for perspective, during my very first quarter at UCLA back in fall of '86, my relatives expressed that

162

they wanted to see me. It had been some years since they had last seen me so, now that I was back in L.A., they wanted me to visit them. I asked them if they could pick me up to which they said it was more convenient for them if I took the city bus. Upon my arrival at a bus stop in the San Fernando Valley, I was to call them from a nearby payphone, collect, stating my location as my name; "You have a collect call from 'Victory and Sepulveda', will you accept the charges?". They would hang up so as not to incur any charges, get in the car, and pick me up from there. I reluctantly did so. After visiting for a few hours — it was about 9:00 o'clock at night — they asked me when the last bus going to UCLA leaves. I asked if they could give me a ride instead, after all, it was only about eight miles away and rush hour was over. They reiterated how it was more convenient for them to simply take me back to the bus stop. I went on to say that taking the bus wasn't possible because I didn't have the fare. They asked how much the fare was and how much money I had. They then gave me exact change to cover the difference. Talk about dysfunctional selfish parsimony. You can pick you friends but you can't pick your relatives. Yet another story for another time.

Anyway, my departure time was approaching and, moreover, I was eager to get back home and salvage as much of my winter break as possible. However, I didn't bring my Walkman with me when I embarked on this adventure so I was also very much dreading being without music for the duration of this bus trip.

Jay said, "How 'bout I go with you to the bus station."

"I'm afraid you'll hafta say your goodbyes here. I'll be headin' into the office right after I drop Mark off."

"Well, Jay, I guess this is it 'n' shit. You take care and hope to see you around sometime."

"You too, man. Thanks again for everything. I really mean that. I would've never made it here without you and sorry again for not levelin' with you from the beginning."

"Hey, man, don't sweat it. What are friends for? Mary, thank you for your hospitality and puttin' up with us unexpected house guests."

"Thank you too, Mark. And Merry Christmas. You're welcome here anytime."

I gathered my things and walked with Richard to his car. I only had one soft-sided duffle-shaped bag which easily fit into the backseat. I got into Richard's car, looked over at the house and waved as we drove off. Jay's Firebird was still parked in the driveway.

Richard and I chitchatted a bit during the half-hour drive to the main bus depot in Indianapolis. Once we got there he got the ticket from the counter, gave it, along with a $20.00 bill, to me, "Here you go. This should cover your meals along the way."

We thanked each other and bid farewell. He left and I was now alone with a depot full of despots. I had some time to kill before the bus would be ready for boarding, so, I strolled around downtown Indianapolis for a bit. I don't recall anything remarkable. It was like most any other big city downtown where a bus depot is located. It was bleak, dirty, kinda rundown, reminiscent of a once thriving metropolis which had since been abandoned for the greener pastures of the suburbs and left behind to decay like the Walkman you forgot about in your closet that you neglected to take the batteries out of. The only thing lacking from this scene of urban blight was that odor which I call the downtown armpit smell. It's like a full dumpster behind a cafeteria that should've been emptied a couple of days ago mixed with diesel exhaust, stale beer and urine. I suspect the lack of that smell may have been due to the fact that it was winter and overcast. The sun hadn't had the opportunity to ferment the muck in the city's gutters to add that certain *je ne sais quoi* to the already pungent palette of odors.

On my way back to the depot, I stopped off to grab some lunch so I wouldn't be hungry on the bus.

'I wonder what kind of mental cases are gonna be on this bus?', I thought to myself.

Finally, the bus was ready to be boarded. I remember it being pretty full. I chose a window seat on the driver's side next to an elderly chick and stowed my bag in the overhead compartment. I would've preferred the aisle but beggars can't be choosers. 'I sure hope she's not some sort of crazy cat lady', I thought to myself. I cautiously took a deep breath through my nose then thought, 'I don't smell cat piss… That's a good sign. I wonder if she's gonna be next to me all the way to Frisco?'.

Next thing you know, she turned to me and said, "Hi, I'm Dolores."

"Hello, I'm Mark."

"I figure since we're sittin' next to each other for a while… say, where're you headed?"

"Frisco."

"Good. Like I was sayin', since we'll be sittin' next to each other for a while, may as well get acquainted, help pass the time."

Well, she's nothing if she's not gregarious. Although I was relieved that she wasn't a militant misanthrope, for all I knew, she could have been a clandestine psycho killer on stabilizing meds. That reminds me of a road trip I took in Australia with an outpatient from a mental institution but that's another story for another time. Nevertheless, I was dreading this trip a little less now. Who knows, maybe it will even be interesting.

* * *

The driver closed the door to the bus, released the brakes with a characteristic hiss of air, then the bus started moving, making its way out the depot onto the local streets toward the interstate. We eventually found ourselves on I-70, the same road Jay and I came in on. It was kinda nice to be seeing the road as a regular passenger rather than a navigator. Don't you remember the slogan on the Greyhound commercials, "Leave the Driving to Us"?

Remember me saying how roughly 90% of a road trip consists of driving with the other 10% being the actual cool stuff you remember? Well, a long bus ride is more like 99% of sitting on a bus watching scenery go by and the occasional meal/rest stops with about 1% of interesting stuff, and I didn't even have any music to listen to. Fortunately for me, Dolores liked to talk and wasn't a half-bad listener either. Most of what we chatted about was idle like the places we lived and countries we visited. While I was talking about my high school career I mentioned I had been in a few musical productions; Bye Bye Birdie, Grease, and Oklahoma. Dolores then said, "That reminds me of the time when I was teaching at a school in New York City back in the 50's and one of my students was Henry Winkler."

"You mean Henry Winkler the actor?"

"Yes, well, he wasn't an actor back then but I could see he was well on his way."

'She seems like she's old enough to have been a teacher back then', I thought to myself.

She went on, "He was in the drama club and they were doing a production of..."

I can't remember the title of the play but I remember that it was a well-known drama that was set on a sailing vessel.

"Near the end, there's a climactic scene where a character is hanged from a yardarm. The drama teacher didn't know how to depict the hanging or even if it was appropriate to do that in the first place, so he directed the kids to simply look up and simultaneously 'react' to a cue. Well, Henry had an idea but he knew it wouldn't be ok'd; like they say, it's easier to get forgiveness than permission. What he did was climb up above the stage where all the lights and rigging are. He scurried over to the rigging that was closest to the curtain and waited for the cue. When the cue came, he tightly held onto the rigging and let his body drop so that his legs would be below the curtain and they could be seen by the audience, and for good measure, he gave his legs a few twitches. The audience let out a gasp and some even screamed."

I thought to myself, 'That's a really cool idea, I'll have to remember that.'

Mary went on, "He got into some serious trouble for that but that was the most memorable production they'd ever had."

I've never been able to verify that story but it doesn't matter; it's a good story. This trip wasn't a one-way ticket to Sucksville after all.

It was getting dark outside and we stopped for a meal. It was snowing and pretty cold. Back on the bus, Dolores and I were talking some more. Eventually, the hum of the engine and gentle rocking of the bus lulled her to sleep. I usually have more difficulty sleeping on a bus than a car. I just can't get comfortable enough on a bus. Besides, regardless of how "nice" Dolores *appeared*, if she were a psycho killer on meds and if they wore off while I was asleep, I could have woken up dead. Anyway, I started to reminisce about my adventure on the Green Tortoise; the music playing on the stereo and the bunks to sleep comfortably...

One of the times I was looking out the window into the inky blackness, I saw a lone patrol car on the eastbound side of the interstate with its bubblegum lights on wondering who he was chasing. I could tell from his headlights that the snow was kinda heavy. Then it looked as though the snow suddenly got really deep. I quickly realized that he had slid off the road into the median.

'Must suck to be you', I thought right then. It hadn't occurred to me that the road the bus was on may be just as treacherous.

As the bus continued westward, passengers who'd reached their respective destinations disembarked and new passengers embarked to replace those who had left. The further west we went the fewer replacements came on board. I cannot remember where Dolores disembarked. For that matter, I can't remember anything else about the rest of that bus ride. But I do remember replaying the past week in my mind over and over and reflecting on the experience.

I thought about the symbolism of Jay's Firebird vis-à-vis Slavic folklore — UCLA taught its students all sorts of things so we would be "well rounded". By the way, most folks tend to make inaccurate associations between the Firebird and the Phoenix. Just to clear up any misinformation, the *only* thing they have in common is fire. Their respective roles in mythology are very different. Anyway, in a nutshell, Slavs believed that the Firebird signified the beginning of a long and troubled journey, a quest as it were. Well, *that* was certainly true in Jay's case. Jay had simultaneously made two journeys; the physical and the spiritual. Driving to his grandmother's place and his metaphorical rebirth respectively. If one looked at Jay's quest as leaving behind the pile of ashes that was once his life and sojourning toward a flourishing new life at the end of the journey, one could easily draw symbolic parallels to Phoenix mythology. Hmm, Jay's Firebird with the Red Bird package... two birds in one... combining the symbolism of both the Firebird and the Phoenix. Gee, if Pontiac had made that car the "Phoenix" package, I would almost entertain a metaphysical connection.

When left alone with your thoughts for hours on end, your mind can come up with all *sorts* of weird things.

* * *

I don't think I was ever so glad to arrive in Frisco as I was that Wednesday. I gathered my things together, disembarked the bus then went in search of the bus that would take me to Salinas. It would still be

170

a while before it was ready so I found a payphone and called Noah so see if he could pick me up. As I said earlier, Noah lived off Hwy. 68 which becomes South Main Street in Salinas so it was pretty much a straight shot for him to come get me.

"Hello?"

"Hey Noah, what's up?"

"Mark? Is that you?"

"Yeah it is. How's it goin' 'n' shit?"

"Good, man. Where are you?"

"I'm in Frisco."

"Don't you mean 'San Francisco'?"

"Hey! If they can refer to Los Angeles as 'L.A.', I can call San Francisco 'Frisco'."

"Yeah, whatever. What are you doin' there? Have you been there since that chase in Salinas?"

"Listen, man, I don't have much time on this payphone. Can you pick me up at the Greyhound station in Salinas at 5:30 this afternoon?"

"Yeah, man, I can be there. So, have you been in San Francisco this whole time?"

"Nah, I'm only changin' busses here. Listen, I'll tell you all about it when you pick me up, ok? I gotta go before the phone cuts me off."

"Ok, man. See ya soon."

"See ya."

Alright. My ride was arranged, I knew where the bus would be, and next I needed some eats. Bus depot food is actually worse than interstate truck stop food but not by much. Don't get me wrong. Greasy spoons and dive restaurants prepare some of the best comfort food you'll ever encounter but bus depot food is like... try to imagine a restaurant run by 7-eleven or run by a theater concession. For one thing, there's no competition so there aren't many choices. Without competition, there's no incentive to do well and that lack of incentive is reflected in the quality of the food they prepare. I'm not saying I won't eat there but I'll only eat there if that's my only option. So, I ate just enough so I wouldn't be hangry by the time I arrived in Salinas.

* * *

I was in the home stretch of my own *There and Back Again* journey when I boarded the bus to Salinas. The depot in Frisco was in an area of the city I was not familiar with but once we got on the freeways, I got my bearings. Every time I went home regardless of which direction I was coming from, I had the same feelings of familiarity and anticipation. Each recognizable landmark we passed let me know we were just that much closer. As we pulled into the bus stop in Salinas, I noticed Noah's Camaro in the parking lot. I grabbed my bag, rushed off the bus and spotted Noah.

"Hey, Mark. Welcome back."

"Thanks man. You have *no* idea how *good* it is to be back."

"Your chariot awaits."

I put my bag in the backseat of the Camaro, sat in the passenger seat, then closed the door. Noah got in and closed his door.

"Where to, sir?"

"I don't know about you but I'm *starved*. How 'bout we go to Roundtable and have Smurf make us a big-ass pizza 'n' shit? I'll even buy."

"Say no more."

And with that he started up the car and we were off.

"How 'bout puttin' on some tunes, man? I haven't heard any music in two-and-a-half days."

"Of course."

This would be the perfect time for *Coming Home* by The Scorpions to have been on the radio.

"So I'm dyin' to know what you've been doin' the past week?"

"Dude, you won't *believe* all the shit that went down and what all I've been through, but, not tryin' to be a dick 'n' shit, I kinda wanna tell it to you and Smurf at the same time since you're both part of it. But until then, how about you tell me what's been goin' on here? How was your Christmas?"

Noah brought me up to date on everything while we took the usual route out of Salinas toward Fort Ord, then through Marina to get on Hwy. 1, then exited at Del Monte / Fremont Blvd. where about a mile or so down, Roundtable was on the left side. That location is now a Japanese restaurant and Roundtable is now on the other side of Fremont Blvd. Noah parked in the lot then we went inside where we saw Smurf.

He looked over and said, "Mark! You're here?"

I smiled and stretched my arms out with my hands facing up like, 'Tada!'

"Where've you *been*, man? What happened after Salinas?"

"Fix me a pizza and I'll tell you all about it."

Smurf knew what kind of pizza I liked and went about making it. Meanwhile, Noah and I got a couple of drinks and sat down at one of the tables.

Smurf brought the pizza when it was ready and sat with us then asked, "So, dude, where've you been the past week?"

"*Guys*, have I got a story to tell *you*."

Where Are They Now?

This part of the story reminds me of the opening verses of Don McLean's *American Pie*: "A long long time ago, I can still remember how that music used to make me smile..."

Oh how we've evolved over the last 34 years.

Jay stayed in Indiana. He never put in the effort to keep in touch. I kinda wonder if his lack of communication with us may have reflected the way he coped with having completely disassociated himself from the life he lead before and all the unpleasant memories and reminders that went with it. Not just turning the page of a book but closing the book and leaving it behind on a shelf in the reading room in a random youth hostel, never to be visited again. Eric put a lot of effort to stay connected with Jay and told me that he had sold the Firebird not long after this adventure; current whereabouts unknown — perhaps it was time for the "Phoenix" Firebird to guide some other lost soul on their road to discovery. Last Eric heard, around 2015 or so, Jay was still in Indiana, got married then divorced.

Eric moved from Clay Center to Abilene a few months after that Christmas and is now in Wichita.

Ever since he moved to Kansas, he's been telling Brett and me how much he misses us and California, and that he'll be coming out to see us soon. We're still waiting.

Brett went to Fresno State then had a successful career in law enforcement; I didn't hold that against him though. He's currently enjoying his retirement and moved to Texas. His Honda actually belonged to his father. In 1989, after the second engine blew, his parents wouldn't financially help him repair it again so his father donated it to a local high school with an auto shop. The car's ultimate fate is unknown.

Smurf and Martin completely disappeared. Nearest I can figure is their fathers got transferred overseas and they never followed up with staying in touch. Being an Army brat, I lost contact with more friends that way than I can remember.

Noah was my closest and most trusted friend. You know how you have "friends" who are nothing more than acquaintances you may see at parties or night clubs and you don't have their phone number and they don't have yours. Then you have "fair weather" friends who you hang out with at their house or your house and you go to parties and clubs with but are nowhere to be found when you need help. Then you have good friends who you do that stuff with, maybe even be each other's wingman, and will help you move. Finally, you have the friend who does all that and will help you move bodies, the guy you can count on no matter what, through thick and thin. That describes Noah. He had diabetes which isn't mentioned in the story because he wasn't defined by it. Don't get me wrong, it was a specter that was forever present throughout his life but he didn't let it keep him from living his life. In the years following this adventure, his diabetes claimed a finger then one of his legs, yet his inspirational sense of humor manifested itself when he dressed up as a pirate with a peg leg for Halloween. Tragically, his diabetes ultimately won out... During his last year, he was no longer able to drive and made the heart wrenching decision to sell his beloved Camaro. I last spoke to his parents some ten years ago; we reminisced and they told me the buyer of Noah's Camaro was in Salinas but they didn't know anything beyond that, let alone the car's current whereabouts.

Mario graduated UCLA then did odd white-collar jobs here and there. He was also the kind of friend who would help you move bodies. A few years after he graduated, he got caught up in a pyramid scheme and sent me an invitation to a free investment seminar presentation. As he was describing the event he had invited me to, it was sounding very sketchy, almost too good to be true. Yet, he was the guy I could count on when the chips were down and he could count on me to support him no matter what. The long and short of it is this seminar was a really finely polished recruitment tool to draw naïve unsuspecting suckers into their pyramid scheme. I realized it within the first two minutes but endured the entire hour — or was it two hours? Afterwards, I pulled Mario aside and, starting with, "You know we're family and I'd go to the mat for you, right?", I told him that as his friend, I had a responsibility to let him know when he was involved in something that was self-destructive. I presented my most cogent argument to him that this company was nothing more than a pyramid scheme. Regrettably, it was too late for Mario; he already drank the cool-aid. He hasn't contacted me since.

Compared to the rest of the guys in my crew, I guess you could say that I'm kinda stuck in a time warp. I still live in California, I still have the same car, I even still have some of the same clothes which still fit. Of course, rather than being resistant to change, I prefer to think I found my groove earlier than the rest of the guys and simply stuck with what worked for me. Hey, if it works, why fix it, right? I graduated UCLA earning a degree in chemistry and have been working in the chemical industry ever since. In 1993, I acquired another vintage car; a 1968 Hearse on a Cadillac chassis. I still have that one too.

And there you have it. My real-life adventure going halfway across country in a stolen Firebird. By the way, did I ever tell you about the time when...

Made in the USA
Middletown, DE
25 February 2022

61807202R00109